Advance Praise for Old Friend from Far Away

"If you are a new writer with a memoir in mind, then Natalie Goldberg's *Old Friend from Far Away* will start your creative engine and get you going. If you are a writer who has lost your concentration and writing rhythm, *Old Friend* will help center and re-inspire you. In this book, Natalie shares her heart and her overflowing spirit."

> —Lee Gutkind,
> editor and founder of *Creative Nonfiction*
> and author of *Forever Fat: Essays by the Godfather*

"Goldberg is a passionate, direct teacher who nurtures creativity in her students as well as a wonderful writer who looks at life straight on. This extraordinary book will inspire readers to remember and write."

> —Marci Shimoff,
> author of *Happy for No Reason*
> and coauthor of *Chicken Soup for
> the Woman's Soul*

"This remarkable book is about life, its richness, its stains, its strangeness, failures, and fun, and how we retrieve it from the hidden part of our imagination through the craft of writing. It is a writers' book written by an extraordinary writer, a book for all of us. Goldberg's wit, intelligence, insight, imagination, and empathy echo through her voice, which catches you again and again in one word: Go! Read it whether you write or not."

> —Joan Halifax, PhD,
> founder and guiding teacher
> of Upaya Zen Center

"Once again, Natalie Goldberg writes in sentences that are so vivid so alive so sumptuous that it makes you want to pick up a pen and do everything she says. And then you do. You pick up the pen, you "go for ten minutes" and suddenly you find yourself returning to what you always knew, to what you thought was lost forever. Through her own writing and her joy-infused writing about writing, you return to yourself. That's a good thing. And Natalie Goldberg should be declared a national treasure."

—Geneen Roth,
author of *The Craggy Hole in My Heart
and the Cat Who Fixed It*

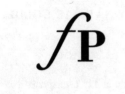

ALSO BY NATALIE GOLDBERG

MEMOIR

The Great Failure: My Unexpected Path to Truth
Long Quiet Highway: Waking Up in America
Living Color: A Writer Paints Her World

POETRY

Top of My Lungs: Poems and Paintings
Chicken and in Love

WRITING BOOKS

Writing Down the Bones: Freeing the Writer Within
Wild Mind: Living the Writer's Life
Thunder and Lightning: Cracking Open the Writer's Craft

NOVEL

Banana Rose

NOTEBOOK

Essential Writer's Notebook

Old Friend from Far Away

The Practice of Writing Memoir

NATALIE GOLDBERG

FREE PRESS

New York   London   Toronto   Sydney

In Memorium Joe Hoar and Peggy French

*f*P

FREE PRESS
A Division of Simon & Schuster
1230 Avenue of the Americas
New York, NY 10020

First Free Press hardcover edition November 2007

FREE PRESS and colophon are registered trademarks of Simon & Schuster, Inc.

For information about special discounts for bulk purchases,
please contact Simon & Schuster Special Sales at 1-800-456-6798
or business@simonandschuster.com

Manufactured in the United States of America

1   3   5   7   9   10   8   6   4   2

Library of Congress Cataloging-in-Publication Data
Goldberg, Natalie.
Old friend from far away : the practice of writing memoir / by Natalie Goldberg.
p.   cm.
Includes bibliographical references.
1. English language—Rhetoric—Study and teaching.   2.
Autobiography—Authorship—Problems, exercises, etc.   I. Title.
PE1479.A88.G63   2008
808'.06692—dc22   2007028270

ISBN-13: 978-1-4165-3502-7
ISBN-10:   1-4165-3502-0

Thank you Mesa Refuge

Thank you
Sky and tree
Big and small
Green and red

The taste of chocolate
Bread and pinto bean

This land and other lands

Past and future
Human, dog and zebra

Everything you know—
And the things you don't

Hunger, zest, repetition
Homesickness,
Welcome.

This is for all my students

Contents

Contents

SECTION II

SECTION III

Contents

SECTION IV

Contents

SECTION V

Contents

SECTION VI

Contents

SECTION VII

Contents

Contents

Read this Introduction

There is nothing stiff about memoir. It's not a chronological pronouncement of the facts of your life: born in Hoboken, New Jersey; schooled at Elm Creek Elementary; moved to Big Flat, New York, where you attended Holy Mother High School. Memoir doesn't cling to an orderly procession of time and dates, marching down the narrow aisle of your years on this earth. Rather it encompasses the moment you stopped, turned your car around, and went swimming in a deep pool by the side of the road. You threw off your gray suit, a swimming trunk in the backseat, a bridge you dived off. You knew you had an appointment in the next town, but the water was so clear. When would you be passing by this river again? The sky, the clouds, the reeds by the roadside mattered. You remembered bologna sandwiches made on white bread; you started to whistle old tunes. How did life get so confusing? Last week your seventeen-year-old told you he was gay and you suspect your wife is having an affair. You never liked selling industrial-sized belts to tractor companies anyway. Didn't you once dream of being a librarian or a dessert cook? Maybe it was a landscaper, a firefighter?

Memoir gives you the ability to plop down like the puddle that forms and spreads from the shattering of a glass of milk on the kitchen floor. You watch how the broken glass gleams from the electric light overhead. The form of memoir has leisure enough to examine all this.

Memoir is not a declaration of the American success story, one undeviating road, the conquering of one mountaintop after another. The puddle began in downfall. The milk didn't get to the mouth. Whatever your life, it is urging you to record it—to embrace the crumbs with the cake. It's why so many of us want to write memoir. We know the particulars, but what really went on? We want the emotional truths under the surface that drove our life.

In the past, memoir was the country of old people, a looking back, a reminiscence. But now people are disclosing their lives in their twenties, writing their first memoir in their thirties and their second in their forties. This revolution in personal narrative that has unrolled across the American landscape in the last two and a half decades is the expression of a uniquely American energy: a desire to understand in the heat of living, while life is fresh, and not wait till old age—it may be too late. We are hungry—and impatient now.

But what if you are already sixty, seventy years old, eighty, ninety? Let the thunder roll. You've got something to say. You are alive and you don't know for how long. (None of us really knows for how long.) No matter your age there is a sense of urgency, to make life immediate and relevant.

Think of the word: *memoir.* It comes from the French *mémoire.* It is the study of memory, structured on the meandering way we remember. Essentially it is an examination of the zigzag nature of how our mind works. The thought of Cheerios ricochets back to a broken fence in our backyard one Nebraska spring, then hops over to the first time we stood before a mountain and understood kindness. A smell, a taste—and a whole world flares up.

How close can we get? All those questions, sometimes murky and uncomfortable: who was that person that was your mother? Why did you play basketball when you longed to play football? Your head wanted to explode until you first snorted cocaine behind the chain-link fence near the gas station. Then things got quiet and peaceful, but what was that black dog still at your throat?

We are a dynamic country, fast-paced, ever onward. Can we make sense of love and ambition, pain and longing? In the center of our speed, in the core of our forward movement, we are often confused and lonely. That's why we have turned so fullheartedly to the memoir form. We have an intuition that it can save us. Writing is the act of reaching across the abyss of isolation to share and reflect. It's not a diet to become skinny, but a relaxation into the fat of our lives. Often without realizing it, we are on a quest, a search for meaning. What does our time on this earth add up to?

The title *Old Friend from Far Away* comes from the *Analects* by Confucius. We reach back in time to another country. Isn't that what memory is?

> To have an old friend visit
> from far away—
> what a delight!

So let's pick up the pen, and kick some ass. Write down who you were, who you are, and what you remember.

Note to Reader

This book is designed not only for you to read but to drench you in the writing process and in your life of memory. Too often we take notes on writing, we think about writing but never do it. I want you to walk into the heart of the storm, written words dripping off hair, eyelids, hanging from hands.

We hope for a linear method of writing. Do A, B, C, and voilà—your memoir is before you, sprung like a cake from a pan. But look at your life: A often doesn't lead to B or C. And that's what makes it compelling—how things worked out in the wrong places or were a disaster where they were supposed to bring happiness. Even if you managed to narrow your life to one thin line: born, went to school, worked a job from nine to five, saved your money, ate a single lamb chop and baked potato on Saturday night, there were still dreams and nightmares, the gaping hole of death at the end, the sudden unmistakable crush on the woman with pale eyes who worked the register at the employee cafeteria.

And because life is not linear, you want to approach writing memoir sideways, using the deepest kind of thinking to sort through the layers: you want reflection to discover what the real connections are. A bit of brooding, pondering, contemplating, but not in a lost manner. I am asking you to make all this dynamic. Pen to paper gives muscle to your deliberations.

Only writing gives you this second chance. Take it. This is the journey I put people on. This is the one I give you in this book.

Old Friend from Far Away

Go

Writing is an athletic activity. It comes from the whole body, your knees and arms, kidneys, liver, fingers, teeth, lungs, spine—all organs and body parts leaning in with you, hovering in concentration over the page. And just like any other sport, it takes practice. Behind the football we see on TV, the players have put in hundreds of hours before the big game. The muscles of writing are not so visible, but they are just as powerful: determination, attention, curiosity, a passionate heart.

Begin to work those muscles. Just like you'd go to the gym every day, or at least three or four times a week, pick up the pen and do these ten-minute exercises. Choose a cheap notebook, in which you are not afraid to make mistakes. Use a fast pen. Try out different ones. Find what suits you. The mind is faster than the hand. Don't slow the hand down more with a ballpoint or a pencil. Cover both sides of the page.

But I like a pencil, you say.

Then use it.

What about a computer?

Use that if you like. Only know that handwriting and pressing the keys with your fingers are two different physical activities and a slightly different slant of mind comes out from each one. Not better or worse, just different.

But remember: there are no excuses not to write. You can't say, but I'm in the woods and don't have my computer with me. Learn to be comfortable with the most simple tools. What if you can't afford to pay your electric bill? You should still be able to write.

Often people who use a computer at work prefer handwriting for memoir to create a boundary between their professional and personal writing. Many writers I know do handwritten first drafts. Then they take it to the keyboard.

We all initially learn to handwrite. Arm connected to shoulder, chest, heart. Come back to the beginning. But maybe that's not true any more. You might be part of the generation that used a computer as your first way to begin to write. If that's so, then use what you know naturally.

Begin with this topic: "I am looking at" and go for a full ten minutes. Whenever you get stuck, write "I am looking at" again and keep going.

Don't cross out.

Don't worry about punctuation, spelling, grammar.

Be specific. Not car, but Cadillac. Not tree, but sycamore. But don't worry, if you write "bird" instead of woodpecker, you can figure out what kind it was two weeks later when you reread it.

The important thing is to keep your hand moving.

Say what you want to say, not what you think you should say. Trust what you put down, even if the editor or critic inside you says it's wrong or you made a mistake. You have time—give yourself at least two weeks before you evaluate. For now you are working out. Sweat. Keep moving.

Feel free to write the worst junk in America.

Every athlete is clumsy at the beginning. Don't worry. Keep going.

When you finish your ten minutes, wind down with your last sentence.

Draw a line under it. Skip a few spaces to begin another ten minutes. Writers are responsible to trees. You don't need to change to a fresh page. As a matter of fact, you also don't need to stay within the margins. We are not in school. You can break the lined structure

Does your hand hurt—or cramp? Shake it out. This is not a race. You just want consistent movement. Don't clutch the pen. Hold it loosely. Keep your writing elbow leaning on the table. If you are writing in your lap, keep your lower arm in a straight line with hand and pen. Relax. Give your wrist support. Have it on the page.

Go for a second ten minutes. Try beginning this one with: "I'm thinking of." Every time you get stuck, come back to the topic "I'm thinking of" as a jump-off.

When you begin your timed writing, you enter your own mind. "I'm thinking of" is a way to begin, to help face the blank page. Once you start, you are on your own, but these two topics—*I'm thinking of; I'm looking at*—are basic, good beginnings. They seem similar, but each is a slightly different way to slice open your mind. When you begin with "I'm thinking of," you lodge yourself more up in the brain. "Looking at" directs you more visually and outwardly. Of course, once you get going they often cross paths. You can return to each one over and over in your exploration of memoir.

A dancer doesn't practice a kick one time in one day and consider that practice to be finished. Keep these topics in your back pocket and exercise them often.

I Remember

Now begin with "I remember" for ten minutes and see where it takes you.

"I remember" hits smack-dab into the heart of memoir. It can produce a smattering of unconnected memories; for instance, I remember long low blue Buicks, Jane's dress, big feet, horses in a field, cucumbers, helicopters, applesauce, Victrolas, yellow chalk, knapsacks—or you might sink into one memory of your father that fills your full ten minutes.

Why do any other topic? you ask. This is it.

Because memory doesn't work so directly. You need to wake up different angles. You might stub your toe one morning and your mind tumbles back to an old friend, who wrote poems, and introduced you one May to peonies. The buds secreted a sticky sweet juice that attracted ants. The ants crawled in and opened the big petals. The flowers couldn't do it on their own, he said. With the sharp ache of your big toe, you remember everything about him. He died too young. You cry from the bottom of a dark well you didn't know you had.

You can't will a memory. Sure, you can doggedly recall details, but the true moment when the details merge with feeling—when the scene is alive—cannot be artificially born. It's like combing the ocean, calling up an abyss—you don't know what you will receive.

Let your mind first believe you are dedicated, that you sincerely want the truth, are willing to take what comes through. Keep moving the pen. Keep practicing.

Who and what you are will come to you. You cannot go after it. When you see something you want, take three steps back and wait.

This does not mean you should lie down and go to bed. "Be submissive to everything, open, listening," author Jack Kerouac urges us. This is a wide state of alertness.

If you want it to snow, that is not a passive occurrence. You must let the sky know you want it and make room in your heart. Then hope your land gets snow, rather than a shower of pebbles or a storm of empty wind.

"Accept loss forever," Kerouac also entreats us. Even a harder, deeper submission.

But forget all this for now. Get to work. Ten minutes. *I remember.* Go.

Test I

Here is a test. The good thing about it is all answers are correct. Right off the top you receive an A.

You have two or three minutes to answer each question. Make sure you are specific. Nothing vague. You might want to begin each answer with "I remember."

_____The first one: give me a memory of your mother, aunt, or grandmother. If it's an aunt say her name; for example, "I remember my aunt Gladys . . ." Be detailed. Here is a beginning example from my own life:

> I remember my mother bit the left corner of her lip when she was nervous. She wore red Revlon lipstick and when she ate Oreos the crumbs stuck to the lipstick. I always recall her lips first. She had a wide mouth with big teeth and her smile was all I longed for as a child.

_____Give me a memory of the color red. Do not write the word "red" but use words that engender the color red when you hear them. For example: a ruby, a tomato, fire, blood.

Writing has the elegance of mathematics. Try to write economically. A red cherry is redundant. Cherry is enough, unless it's one of the yellow ones from Washington State. Then it's a yellow cherry. But, otherwise, cherry immediately wakes up the color red in the mind.

Test I

Here's an example:

I remember I dug radishes out of the garden in late fall and then lay by the side of the creek watching the rose sunset spread out through the clouds. At the last minute, just before the sun dropped behind the horizon, it flamed up, a perfect crimson ball.

Besides referring to "rose sunset," "crimson," and "flamed" for red, I also threw in radishes, another red item, for fun.

_____Give me a memory of sound. Again try not to use the word "sound" in your writing. Here's an example:

I remember hearing the lawn mower as I lay in bed when I was twelve, reading *Gone with the Wind* and listening to Joan Baez on the hi-fi. I liked music and reading at the same time, but the noise outside bugged me.

Note the verbs "hearing" and "listening" connote sound. Of course, also the nouns "noise" and "music." What other words can be used?
Go: you have two to three minutes.

_____Give me a picture of a teacher you had in elementary school.

You don't remember any one of them? Try to recall their names. How tall was Mrs. Schneider? Slowly creep inside your memory bank. You are not sure if she wore an orange or blue dress—pick one color and keep going. The more we exercise the act of remembering, even if we are not one hundred percent certain, the more will come clear. Ask with a big shout. A big answer will come back.

Oh, yes, I remember my second grade teacher better. Miss McCall. Short hair, straight bangs and a space between her front teeth. She wore gray every day. I am almost certain of this. And there was a glass of water on her desk. I never saw her drink from it but sometimes it was suddenly empty.

_____Another one: Tell me about a meal you loved. Where were you when you ate it? What was the weather like out the window? Who were you with? How old were you?

Eating is a good study. No matter how asleep we might be in our lives, we manage to wake up and remember a good meal. Did you leave anything on the plate? Were there flowers on the table? Paper napkins? Did you have seconds?

Are you stumped? Begin with: I don't remember anything about that meal except . . .

_____One more: Tell me about a time you remember rain. Rain might not be the main focus of a memory but write about a time when it was there with you as you said good-bye to your grandmother one cold day in November or kissed your first girlfriend on the lips before school at eight a.m.

Okay, what am I teaching you here—besides detail, besides getting your mind to roam over different territory? Can you guess?

I'm teaching you to use your senses when you write. Sound, taste, touch, sight. I didn't specifically mention a smell.

Right now list ten smells you remember. Be specific.

bacon
wisteria
smoke
piñon sap
the ocean
Bazooka bubblegum
a new book

toothpaste
vomit
grass fertilizer

Naturally, you are not going to cover every sense every time you write a scene:

"I liked her. She smelled like roses. She tasted like alfalfa. She sounded like a saxophone and she felt like a horse's mane and looked like the devil."

See how ridiculous that is? can we take this out?

But doing this "I Remember" test is like acupuncture pricks, alerting your mind when you write. You go along describing something and then—ah, yes, *Snow was falling wet as my heart when I asked her to marry me.* The world becomes bigger. Your love includes weather now—and feeling.

No One Has Ever Died

Now give me ten minutes of "I don't remember." Another approach is: "I forget," but "I don't remember" is right on target. The direct opposite.

How can you remember what you don't remember? You are calling out to empty space for help, to the underbelly, to the things you don't want to remember. To remember we have to look back. This assignment is asking you to look back at the back—if that makes sense. If it doesn't, don't worry about it. To write you have to let go of common sense. Levelheadedness only leads to a chastising of yourself—this whole idea of writing a memoir is a dumb idea. You should be earning a living, buying new clothes for that interview. Make an eye exam appointment. Get your head examined.

Digging up the dark world, the things you don't remember, releases a lot of energy. Bring to light things that have been covered up for a long time and they snap and crackle. Usually we try to control what we remember. Control leads to dull writing.

Another rule for writing practice: lose control. Let the mute, the silent speak. Your memoir should be a large field, capable of embracing whatever comes up. If you avoid a corner or crag, the reader will feel it.

No one has ever died of writing in her notebook what is hidden or dangerous. You might cry—or laugh—but not die.

After I said this once in a class, a student came right up into my face: I want to be the first to die of writing practice.

You go, girl.

But for the meek rest of us, worry later about your fears—what your mother, brother, partner, co-workers, father, priest, even your angel will think. For now get it out on the page. Discover what you are so fiercely hiding or not remembering or blanking out on.

First masturbation, who you had a crush on, thoughts of leaving, of travel, of another person's lover, of revenge. All kinds of experiences that are yours and no one else's. What you saw your sister do, a time you saw your mother sneak off with another man, how your father behaved in a bar. These are your thoughts and memories. Yet there are consequences if the wrong person reads them.

I have heard many stories of a parent, a teacher, a friend reading something and the shame, the crisis, the confusion that ensued.

First, let's say, you have a right to write what you want. You will never get any further in writing if you censor your life.

Can you imagine a memoir based on protection?

I had a good life.
It was pretty.
It was very interesting.
It was nice.
I played cards.
I swam.
I worked at my job.
I got married and had three children.
I'm going to die.

And the next line would be: Yipeee! Then I can stop writing this. But you probably wouldn't even mention death. It's not polite.

We have to go to the next step. If what you write is frightening to you, tear it up, burn it, after you are done.

Then write it again. Destroy it.

Then write it again. And chew it up and swallow.

Build a tolerance for what you cannot bear. This is good practice. It makes your capacity larger. You grow and are willing to embrace more. Your memoir becomes richer.

But also find a good hiding place for your notebook. It's no one's business.

This is the beginning: to let out what you have held hidden.

Here's another rule of writing practice: Go for the jugular, for what makes you nervous. Otherwise, you will always be writing around your secrets, like the elephant no one notices in the living room. It's that large animal that makes your living room unique and interesting. Write about it. There is such relief in acknowledging what you mistrust, how you have been hurt, the way you see the world differently from your teachers or parents. Let's not even worry for now whether what you write will be in your memoir. Get it out and down on the page. If you don't, you'll keep tripping over it.

Make a list of all the things you should not write about. Yes, then, of course, systematically go down the list and let it rip. Ten minutes on each one.

You will want your memoir to have tension and drive, to let people know you were alive on this earth. This willingness to write with fear and danger at your side is the beginning of how you give your writing a friction that draws in your reader. They will trust you.

Because there is so much dread about what someone else thinks, I want to repeat this:

You have a right to write it.
Throw it out, rip it up, swallow it down.
Build up a capacity to bear up—don't let fear run your writing life.
Hide your notebook in a good place.

In real life get out of the way when a person with a gun is running down the street. In your writing life step in front of his path, let him shoot you in the heart.

What you fear, if you turn toward it, will give your writing teeth.

Die

Tell me what you will miss when you die.

Three

Name three times when it came to you clearly that you wanted to write a memoir. Go. Ten minutes.

If it's a true desire: go out and get a few cheap spiral notebooks, some fast-writing pens—and a few writing friends. Meet with them and write. Make a rule, no conversation till you've done two twenty-minute writes. Read what you wrote to each other.

Do you play tennis alone, football, soccer? This writing sport, too, needs pals. You can't do it alone. You write with your own lonely mind—don't make it harder on yourself. Get some friends. Remember when the desire was real to write this memoir? Don't backpedal. Up and down the hills you go.

But how do you meet these people?

You don't find running partners in the movies or lacrosse friends in the grocery. Go to where writers are—lectures, bookstores, libraries, classes, conferences, weekend workshops. Look on bulletin boards for writing groups.

You've never been to a reading before? There is always a first time.

During a question-and-answer session after a reading, a woman declared: "I am eighty-seven and never thought to come to one of these before." She threw up her hands. "I love it. I love it. Whoever thought to hear a writer read aloud in her own words."

Don't wait till you are almost ninety. Go now.

Coffee

Tell me about how you drink coffee. When? Where?

If you don't drink it, tell me how you stopped. Tell me about its smell and the half-drunk cups you notice on tables next to yours in a café. The cream or milk, the spoon, the sugar, the cup itself. I bet you know more about coffee than the person drinking it. Write about it now. Ten minutes. Go.

When I lived in the Midwest, people invited: "Come for coffee," which usually meant a weak brew backed up by home-made bars, walnut bread, cookies, often on a tablecloth, even with silver laid out.

A whole world exists in coffee. Glean those details. Everything you know about coffee. Go. Ten minutes.

Tell Me

Tell me everything you know about Jell-O. Go. Ten minutes. Let it rip.

Dishes

Tell me about a time you washed the dishes. Go. Ten minutes.

Jean Rhys

When was the first time you were afraid? Write for ten minutes.

When was the last time you were happy, really happy? Write for ten minutes.

In her novel *After Leaving Mr. Mackenzie,* Jean Rhys, an English author, has her character Julia musing about these very questions of fear and happiness.

You are writing a memoir, not a novel, but don't limit where you can find inspiration. A shoe, a knock on the door, the middle line of a sonnet, the ripple of a horse's shank, your very own steering wheel can set your mind spinning. This is not the beginning of dementia. It's the beginning of love. A connection that sets you reeling.

And you could remember the first time you were afraid.

You were walking along a long path, shadowed for some distance by trees. But at the end of the path was an open space and the glare of white sunlight. You were catching butterflies. You caught them by waiting until they settled, and then creeping up silently on tiptoe and squatting near them. Then, when they closed their wings, looking like a one-petalled flower, you grabbed them quickly, taking hold low down or the wings would break in your hand.

When you had caught the butterfly you put it away in an empty tobacco tin, which you had ready. And then you walked along, holding the tin to your ear and listening to the sound of the beating of wings against it.

It was a very fascinating sound. You wouldn't have thought a butterfly could make such a row.

Besides, it was a fine thing to get your hand on something that a minute before had been flying around in the sun. Of course, what always happened was that it broke its wings; or else it would fray them so badly that by the time you had got it home and opened the box and hauled it out as carefully as you could it was so battered that you lost all interest in it. Sometimes it was too badly hurt to be able to fly properly.

"You're a cruel, horrid child, and I'm surprised at you."

And, of course, you simply did not answer this. Because you knew that what you had hoped had been to keep the butterfly in a comfortable cardboard box and to give it the things it liked to eat. And if the idiot broke its own wings, that wasn't your fault, and the only thing to do was to chuck it away and try again. If people didn't understand that, you couldn't help it.

That was the first time you were afraid of nothing—that day when you were catching butterflies—when you had reached the patch of sunlight. You were not afraid in the shadow, but you were afraid in the sun.

The sunlight was still, desolate, and arid. And you knew that something huge was just behind you. You ran. You fell and cut your knee. You got up and ran again, panting, your heart thumping, much too frightened to cry.

But when you got home you cried. You cried for a long time; and you never told anybody why.

The last time you were happy about nothing; the first time you were afraid about nothing. Which came first?

Rhys doesn't try to clinch it: I was scared because the butterflies died or because I was yelled at or because everything didn't go my way. She lets things be opaque, nuanced. This is big writing. It's not bad to leave a touch of ambiguity.

But vagueness is another story. Don't hide from the truth, afraid to address it. Rhys allowed the largeness of the situation. Fear—or happiness—can't be reduced to one quick answer.

But I'm writing a memoir about baseball, you say. Who needs this fear and happiness stuff? I want to play ball.

These explorations will enrich your baseball memoir, so it won't be limited to a list of scores you remember, who was on base, what the ump said. Why the hell do you love baseball in the first place? Why should we come along with you? Link it to that hunger and edge of desire that drew you to that hard ball. Let your memoir be rich in feelings. Even baseball has more going on than one good game.

The Four-Letter Word

Let's dare talk about love for a moment, shall we?

Being in love is a loss of control. Suddenly your life is dependent on the eyebrow twitch of Joe Schmo. It's terrible—it's thrilling. Everyone wants it.

No one says it but writing induces that state of love. The oven shimmers, the faucet radiates, you die into the mouth that only you see. Right there, sitting with your notebook on your lap, even the factory town you drove through heading north to Denver, the town you hated and prayed no flat tire, no traffic jam would hold you there, even that place while writing about that trip, that day, that year, you caress now. Your life is real. It has texture, detail. Suddenly it springs alive.

Hardly moving, only the pen, hand, wrist, lower arm in a quiet stir, yet love is exuding from your every cell. You are like a great mountain, a buddha. You are yourself.

Tell me about a breakfast you were once privileged to have. Eggs over easy? Grapefruit? One thin slice of toast? Not even that. You ate a pickle—and it never tasted so good. You vowed to eat pickles for breakfast for the rest of your life. Then what happened? Tell me. Be specific. Go. Ten minutes.

Ugly

Tell me what you thought was ugly. Be detailed. Go. Ten minutes.

Home

Where is home for you? Go. Ten minutes

Peach

What a writer really does is fall in love with an author and read everything he or she has written. In doing so, you realize your own soul and the author's are akin. It makes you want to communicate outwardly, to share your own feelings and observations back. Reading this favorite author opens you. Then after you absorb the entire work, you go on to someone else. This stretches you.

It's a simple idea really: eat a lot of peaches, you'll become a peach. Read good books, ones that are well-written where the author cares, thinks, is willing to feel the aching texture of the world and of his own rough mind and you are at least a third of the way into the practice.

List ten memoirs you want to read. Don't know of ten? Go to the bookstore and browse. Go to the library and run your finger along the stacks full of memoirs.

Plan to go down your list and read each book on it. It's your assignment. You can't read the prologue and decide to quit.

If you are an Armenian American, it's good to read other Armenians. It supports your voice and helps to give a confidence in your experience.

But don't stop there. Stretch yourself to read other possibilities: Chinese Americans, Koreans, Filipinos, Africans, French. Let books take you beyond your comfort level. You might discover something about yourself from a whole new angle. Going away sometimes brings us home.

In Paris, Hemingway was able to find his Michigan and

write about it. In that same City of Light Saul Bellow found his Chicago and wrote *Augie March.*

Authors we read are our mentors. We study the author's mind—how she presents her work—and it informs us of possible ways to write.

James Baldwin

Here are the opening paragraphs of an essay entitled "Notes of a Native Son." I want you to read them out loud. If possible read them to another person. The act of having another human being listening intensifies words; they reverberate back to you, inside you.

Listen also to what is not said. It is a listening not just with your ears—though ears are a fine thing—but listening with your whole body, with your heart and the hairs on your arms and the small toes of your feet. Try doing it this way when you read James Baldwin, one of our very great American writers, out loud:

On the 29th of July, in 1943, my father died. On the same day, a few hours later, his last child was born. Over a month before this, while all our energies were concentrated in waiting for these events, there had been, in Detroit, one of the bloodiest race riots of the century. A few hours after my father's funeral, while he lay in state in the undertaker's chapel, a race riot broke out in Harlem. On the morning of the 3rd of August, we drove my father to the graveyard through a wilderness of smashed plate glass.

The day of my father's funeral had also been my nineteenth birthday. As we drove him to the graveyard, the spoils of injustice, anarchy, discontent, and hatred were all around us. It seemed to me that God himself had devised, to mark my father's end, the most sustained and brutally dissonant of codas. And it seemed to me, too, that the violence which rose all about us as my father left the world had been devised as a corrective for the pride of his eldest son. I had declined to believe in that apocalypse which had been central to my father's vision; very well, life seemed to be saying, here is something that will certainly pass for an apocalypse until the real thing comes along. I had inclined to be contemptuous of my father for the conditions of his life, for the conditions of our lives. When his life had ended I began to wonder about that life and also, in a new way, to be apprehensive about my own.

I had not known my father very well. We had got on badly, partly because we shared, in our different fashions, the vice of stubborn pride. When he was dead I realized that I had hardly ever spoken to him. When he had been dead a long time I began to wish I had. It seems to be typical of life in America, where opportunities, real and fancied, are thicker than anywhere else on the globe, that the second generation has no time to talk to the first. No one, including my father, seems to have known exactly how old he was, but his mother had been born during slavery. He was of the first generation of free men. He, along with thousands of other Negroes, came North after 1919 and I was part of that generation which had never seen the landscape of what Negroes sometimes call the Old Country.

He had been born in New Orleans and had been a quite young man there during the time that Louis Armstrong, a boy, was running errands for the dives and honky-tonks of what was always presented to me as one of the most wicked of cities—to this day, whenever I think of New Orleans, I also helplessly think of Sodom and Gomorrah. My father never mentioned Louis Armstrong, except to forbid us to play his records, but there was a picture of him on our wall for a long time. One of my father's strong-willed female relatives had placed it there and forbade my father to take it down. He never did, but he eventually maneuvered her out of the house and when, some years later, she was in trouble and near death, he refused to do anything to help her.

28

He was, I think, very handsome. I gather this from photographs and from my own memories of him, dressed in his Sunday best and on his way to preach a sermon somewhere, when I was little. Handsome, proud, and ingrown, "like a toenail," somebody said. But he looked to me, as I grew older, like pictures I had seen of African tribal chieftains: he really should have been naked, with war-paint on and barbaric mementos, standing among spears. He could be chilling in the pulpit and indescribably cruel in his personal life and he was certainly the most bitter man I have ever met; yet it must be said that there was something else in him, buried in him, which lent him his tremendous power and, even, a rather crushing charm. It had something to do with his blackness, I think—he was very black—with his blackness and his beauty, and with the fact that he knew that he was black but did not know that he was beautiful. He claimed to be proud of his blackness but it had also been the cause of much humiliation and it had fixed bleak boundaries to his life. He was not a young man when we were growing up and he had already suffered many kinds of ruin; in his outrageously demanding and protective way he loved his children, who were black like him and menaced, like him; and all these things sometimes showed in his face when he tried, never to my knowledge with any success, to establish contact with any of us. When he took one of his children on his knee to play, the child always became fretful and began to cry; when he tried to help one of us with our homework the absolutely unabating tension which emanated from him caused our minds and our tongues to become paralyzed, so that he, scarcely knowing why, flew into a rage and the child, not knowing why, was punished. If it ever entered his head to bring a surprise home for his children, it was, almost unfailingly, the wrong surprise and even the big watermelons he often brought home on his back in the summertime led to the most appalling scenes. I do not remember, in all those years, that one of his children was ever glad to see him come home. From what I was able to gather of his early life, it seemed that this inability to establish contact with other people had always marked him and had been one of the things which had driven him out of New Orleans. There was something in him, therefore, groping and tentative, which was never expressed and which was buried with him. One saw it most clearly when he was facing new people and hoping to impress them. But he never did, not for long. We went from church to smaller and more improbable church, he found himself in less and less demand as a minister, and by the time he died none of his friends had come to see him for a long time. He had lived and died in an intolerable bitterness of spirit and it frightened me, as we drove him to the graveyard through those unquiet, ruined streets, to see how powerful and overflowing this bitterness could be and to realize that this bitterness now was mine.

Did you notice right off that Baldwin embeds his father's death in other events happening at the same time? The Detroit race riot; another one in Harlem; driving to the graveyard through "smashed plate glass." The birth of his father's youngest child occurred a few hours after his father's death, and the day of the burial was also Baldwin's nineteenth birthday. That awareness of simultaneous events intensifies and enlarges the main event. Nothing happens in a vacuum. Zero in on the most personal detail, step back and see how it is interconnected with public detail.

Let's take Baldwin's paragraphs further. What did you hear in every word he wrote? This is a bit subtler but once it is pointed out you'll recognize it.

Yes, each word had fearless conviction. But where did that come from?

This is what I heard when I read it in Sedona, Arizona, to a group of one hundred and fifty people from twenty-seven states and five provinces of Canada, where not a pin dropped as I uttered Baldwin's words: James Baldwin, the writer, had passed to the other side. He had let go of trying to please—or not please—of getting kudos, credentials, appreciation. He was laying down word after word with an even hand. He was no longer his father's child. He wrote this piece when he was thirty-one; his father died when he was nineteen. But it felt as I read that it wasn't so much that twelve years had passed; rather, that this seeking for truth began a long time before and that he was willing to break any ties that bound him from seeing authentically. In the texture and strength of his words I felt he'd looked death—his death—in the face and decided he'd walk with his maker and no one else. This gave him a freedom of observation, a rare ability to write clearly.

I was so moved that immediately after driving back from the Sedona workshop I hurried over to a bookstore in Santa Fe. A thin volume of Baldwin's fiction was on the shelf: *Giovanni's Room.* I purchased it and the next day flew to Florida to help my ninety-year-old mother. A hurricane had devastated her neighborhood—only a few bedraggled royal palms remained—and her roof leaked.

I read this novel in my mother's back room, lying on the couch, on the floor—in shorts, in a bathing suit. I called roofers; I shopped for food. I hardly noticed the humid morning; then the pounding afternoon rain. My mother called out; she needed to find her glasses. I dragged myself away from the book to minister to her. I was in a trance. Who was this James Baldwin? I'd read *The Fire Next Time* thirty years ago. I'd pigeonholed him as a black writer. Sure, he chronicled a certain time in African American life, but his work reaches beyond definition and category to what is real and essential in human existence. And I was right about my intuition about death: at the end of this book the main character looks it right in the face.

I couldn't believe what was happening to me in southern Florida at my mother's usually mundane retirement community. I was reading one of the most beautiful books of my life.

And here I recall it with great pleasure and humility. To encounter a fine book and have the time to read it is a wonderful thing.

Tell me of a great book you have read. Ultimately, writing won't go far if you have never fallen in love with a book, an author, even the smell of the paper, the sweet anticipation of opening to page one and beginning. In falling in love we realize we are not separate—that that river of words is part of us.

Again

Let's look another time at this worry about writing what people close to you—or people not close to you—will criticize you for. What are you going to do? Walk around with masking tape glued over your mouth? You have to speak. That's why you put the pen in your hand to begin with: in order to not blank out or turn your back. You have to be willing to go into the hot, steamy center, to go to the mat for sorrow, grief, concern, in order to shed light on what has been in shadow.

You might also be holding that pen to discover things that you did not know how to say. And you don't always know, you can't be sure what someone's response will be. You can't write in anticipation and worry. But, yes, people will not always applaud you.

In my last memoir, I wrote about my father and the teacher I'd studied with for twelve years. I loved them both enough to write a whole book, exploring the hard—and good—dimensions of our relationship. A decade earlier I'd written a glowing memoir about the same teacher. Three years after it came out, incidents surfaced that I hadn't known about. I felt a responsibility to complete the story. I didn't point fingers. I wanted to understand. I loved my teacher deeply and I felt betrayed and disappointed. What I felt mattered. What the other students felt mattered, too, but no one was speaking.

A writer's job is to speak. Try to be as careful, as respectful as possible. Check all your facts. Have a measure of equanimity. Part of your clarity comes in the writing.

I dug up all the old addresses and sent out notices to people I had practiced with twenty years ago. Then I flew up in the dead of winter to meet with them to tell them what I was doing. Everyone knew the story—it was no surprise.

But, whatever you do, you cannot prevent trouble. When the book came out, it was met with a wall of silence. No one called to argue, disagree. That would have been a connection. That would have felt good. The experience was painful. I stopped writing for eight months. I didn't trust what I said. I kept opening the book to find the awful thing I had done. It wasn't there. You can't control people's reactions.

And my family? How did they react to what I said about my father? There was a ruffle, a quick forgetting, and a fast movement back to the status quo.

Both men were dead when I wrote the memoir, but you can't always wait for someone to die.

Am I sorry I wrote it? No. With that book, I grew up. It wasn't fun, but I came to a much deeper understanding of where I stood. Writing has to move us. Writing is alive, a living process.

Sometimes you are not willing or ready to reveal things you have written. That's fine. You may never want to, but I'd encourage you to write them down, to examine them, then bury the notebook if you want, but don't let those things pollute your other writing. And they will. Whatever is hidden or secretive will look for a way out. You'll write about a grilled cheese sandwich and bubbling up in the middle of the cheese will be incest, deception, and adultery. Claiming it, exploring it will free you. It doesn't always mean you have to make it public.

You can make choices, but only when your secrets are up front, on the page. When they are at your back, concealed, they can only haunt you.

What's in Front of You

Write what's in front of your face. This is a grounding exercise when your mind is flitting all over. Begin with the most ordinary: *beige carpet, wastebasket, four legs of a wood chair and a white wall. On the wall hangs a jaunty abstract painting of a Buddha and a cat. A white lamp is on the table.*

If something not in front of you comes to mind, jot it down: *An almond butter sandwich I once ate on a hike. I think I put jelly on it too. Strawberry.*

Back to the room: *Black pen on the floor, a folder. Bookshelves piled with spiral notebooks, a box of tissues, a pencil drawing of a head by a young girl named Anne Kadets.*

Go ahead. Let the almond butter come back. *We were in Yellowstone. September. I was no longer young but I was eating that gooey stuff. It was Wyoming. I'd never been there before. I kept repeating: I am in Wyoming. Why oh me.*

Do you see? What is in front of you anchors your mind so when you go off into memory there is weight. You don't just fly around and never land.

Try it. Ten minutes. If no memory comes, then you get good practice in noticing the physical details around you.

Outside

What about a time you slept outside? Tell me about it. Go. Ten minutes.

End

Tell me about how a relationship ended. Go. Ten minutes.

Test II

Let's do some more "I remembers." Three minutes each.

_____Tell me about a time you were in trouble in class.

_____Tell me how you first learned to read.

_____Teach me something. It doesn't have to be the traditional subjects. How about how to tie a shoe, be a good mother, how to clean out the refrigerator, make pudding, change a tire? Something that is deep in your bones—driving in rush hour on I-94 to work each day.

_____Tell me how you felt about math. Don't just say, "I hated it." Write about an experience around it: Counting out change, a math course, a situation in school, using division or multiplication, keeping an expense account—or maybe you are one of the rare ones that keeps a math journal.

_____Tell me some details about an uncle or grandfather. Make sure to name the uncle: "I remember Uncle Phil . . ."

Now, these are short, two- or three-minute searches. If one of them whets your appetite, you can write more later. Have a list of topics in the back of your notebook. Every time you flash on a subject that piques your interest, jot it down. These "I remembers" are mind probes. They cover a lot of territory in a brief amount of time, like driving across the country in two days. Next time you'll stop in a town you liked, have a cup of tea, maybe even move there.

Notice that each request begins with "Tell me." Feel the difference between "Tell about a bicycle you had" and "Tell me about a bicycle you had." It's a little nudge. You have someone—in this case me—you are talking to. It gives your writing a direction. In the act of writing is the unspoken need of having another to listen.

But what about those piles of private journals we keep? Even there we write to speak to another part of ourselves, to explain, to make sense. Don't ever forget that when we write, we want to communicate, share, break through isolation to another human being. Writing has an urgency. Tell me—we won't be here forever.

Funny

Tell me about a funny or odd thing that has happened in or around your car. Go. Ten minutes.

Storage

Tell me about a storage unit or someplace you stored things.
Write for ten minutes.

Third

What is the third thing? There is you and there is writing. But you can't write about writing. It's ingrown. You and writing must gaze out at a third thing. Of course, a fourth, a fifth will appear, but for now the two of you look out together. What is there in this world? Shoes, buttons, dirty snow, another person with his head bent low against the wind. With writing at your side you can see all the way over to Japan, those monks sweeping the leaves, bending their heads over thin warm soup.

Writers don't know that much except how to write. We must find the third thing. And we cannot afford to be fussy. How a pothole is formed holds our interest. A kind of cheese, a license to own a beauty parlor, a felt slipper, someone's toothache, all are fodder for our pen, for our joint rapture with our notebook.

This is true of couples too. They need a third thing—a child, a dog, a house, a business—to gaze upon. Not face to face, but side to side. In his memoir *The Best Day the Worst Day,* about his marriage to Jane Kenyon, Donald Hall writes about this, how they both had poetry together, travel, their friends, their friends' children, Ping-Pong, church, gardening, the shared pleasure of their rural New England community.

What is your third thing? Yes, of course, it can be your memories. Go, for ten minutes.

Steve Almond

Memoirs are not usually about your whole life, covering birth to the present moment. They are more an expression of your life through something. For instance, your childhood in Texas, not just your childhood, but how it evolved in a certain place and time. It's a related record. You didn't shoot up in a void.

You could write about your life with books. Your life as a nerd, as a fry cook, as an addict. Of course, inadvertently it is about your favorite character—you. But it's a better idea not to approach memoir head-on: "I'll tell you everything about myself and you'll love it." I don't think so, as darling as you may be.

"Well, then why should I write this memoir? I knew my life was worthless." You sit with hunched shoulders, a belligerent look on your face.

You have to find the access, the opening, some way the rough elbow of your mind can be revealed, and plunge forth on the page. What am I talking about?

It's best to get concrete as soon as possible. Here's an example: Steve Almond is a serious author who has written hundreds of good short stories about his relationship angsts. He has two collections out, *My Life in Heavy Metal* and *The Evil B.B. Chow and Other Stories*. He's written articles for prestigious publications and teaches creative writing at Boston College.

But it was when he wrote *Candyfreak: A Journey through the Chocolate Underbelly of America* that people paid attention. "The author has eaten a piece of candy every single day of his entire life." He felt foolish when the idea came to him. Candy wasn't

43

serious enough. It wasn't literary. To write about candy was below him. Yet candy was a great passion of his. In a sense he backed into the subject. He wouldn't have logically chosen it.

This is often true of your subject matter. You can't think, okay, I need an angle and try to manipulate the writing system. Writing is smarter—and bigger—than you. Also slipperier. Don't think you can catch the process in your hand and contain it. That's why we love it, long for it, why writing will always be the elusive lover.

Steve Almond wrote about that sweet stuff, and, lo and behold, it was through candy that he actually got heard. But candy? Yes, anything a writer is drawn to and looks into deeply reveals himself. And because, let's admit it, we all care about candy, we suddenly become interested and care about his suffering. Candy illuminated his pain that he'd been trying to share all along.

The main thing, though, is that I formed this emotional bond to candy. My parents were too busy, my older brother wanted me dead, my twin brother set off into the world without me. This was how I saw things. I was a needy kid, and terribly lonely, and candy kept me company. I wasn't fat, but I understood the appeals of gluttony, how a certain frantic gratification might numb the sting of sorrow. And if it seems, at times, that I am playing off my obsession with candy as something frivolous/heartwarming, this is, like most of our routines, just a way of obscuring its darker associations.

I can remember staggering down the streets of Baden-Baden, Germany, at dawn, close to hysterical with an unnamed sadness. This was the summer between my sophomore and junior years in college. I was traveling in Europe because I assumed this was what one did at age 20 in order to acquire that mysterious attribute known as worldliness. Earlier in the day, I'd met some fellow travelers at a hostel and we'd smoked some hash and there was some girl involved, a blond Australian who I hoped might be willing to kiss me a little. But I did something uncool, let my desperation show, and they ditched me outside a fancy casino. I wandered back to the hostel, but it was closed for the night and when I tried to sneak in, a German fellow came and shouted at me in a manner that made me think of Hitler. So I spent the night walking from one end of town to the other. When I think about this episode, what returns to me most vividly is the elegant vending machine outside that casino, which sold Lindt chocolate bars for a single deutsche mark. And how, in the morning, I found an outdoor café and bought a roll which I cut in half and buttered to make a chocolate sandwich.

Years later, I moved to Poland to live with a woman. But we soon fell out of love and began to argue. In the evenings, after our fights, flushed and seething and scared to death, I would wander the narrow avenues of her town and stop at one of the kiosks to buy a candy bar, the name of which I don't remember, only that it was a sweet vanilla wafer covered in a dark, bitter chocolate. On the day I returned home to America, I found a cache of these bars at the bottom of my suitcase, left there by my lover, that I might carry with me, at least a little longer, the taste of our doomed enterprise.

—from *Candyfreak*

In the end he gets to talk about himself in a real way but now it's also connected to something larger—the trail of candy. What's more luminous?

What do you think your passions are? Don't think. Make a list.

Now write for ten minutes, keep the hand going, what are your obsessions? Go.

Tell me this: what's the difference between a passion and an obsession? These are the kinds of questions writers love to ponder. Would you rather have an obsession or a passion?

Hint: obsession is linked to suffering.

Nuts

Think of the history of nuts in your life. Notice: You were not asked how you *feel* about nuts. "The history of nuts" is a slightly different angle, a bit more elevated than "I ate lots of cashews when I watched TV." History demands dates, place, a more distant reflection. How have nuts impacted your life? Memoir is a luxurious long taste. The cashews are fine, but "history" is asking for more depth, a broader look, but it is never an invitation to be only abstract. You must make sure to plant in specifics. And of course "history of nuts" can also be the nutty friends, co-workers, lovers—you name it—you've encountered.

Tell me about your *romance* with chocolate. An *incident* with vanilla. Give me a *journal page* of your experience with tapioca—or rice pudding. Bread pudding more like it? Go for it.

Let's look at some other good words to use:

donut confessions
the public record of my pie eating
chronicle of croissants
pudding diary
my sugar archives
coffee ice cream accounts
the narrative of my sweet life
a roster of caramel tarts I've eaten

These are fresh ways to record things. We think of dessert as frivolous. Juxtaposing "annals" with chocolate chip cookies gives it humor—and seriousness. Why shouldn't sweets have a lofty title?

But, of course, this can be used in other ways: report of my bad teeth, lousy day recital, episodes with mice, my legendary dog, the saga of my ill will.

Adding a strong noun in the front or back of your topic cracks open your mind to different ways of seeing the usual: my belief in paper clips.

Grade

Tell me everything you remember about kindergarten. Don't remember much? You know what to do. Begin from there. Go. Ten minutes.

Fifteen years ago I taught a workshop in Washington, D.C., and I assigned *third grade* for the topic. People raised their hands to read what they had written. The fourth person had an accent, but read evenly and matter-of-factly: "I did not go to third grade. At that age I was in Bergen-Belsen . . ." He went on to list what he would have been learning then—multiplication, conjunctions, apostrophes—but he didn't learn them. He didn't describe the conditions at the concentration camp, and he didn't need to. We felt its hollow ring in everything not said. He wasn't trying to be artistic when he wrote. He merely listed the things he did not learn. The effect on us was profound. No one spoke or raised a hand after he was finished. For him the facts of his life were the facts of his life. We had heard of the horror of the camps but to distill it down to a loss of third grade grammar and history had a startling effect. We felt the pain in a new way. Not by what happened but by the simple things that didn't happen.

What did not happen in your sixth grade? Be specific. You can also step out of the ordinary confines of curriculum. You were eleven or twelve. What was missing? Go. Ten minutes.

No Mush

In order to write we must have an awareness of who we are—
and who we aren't. If you don't know either, writing can help
teach it.

Know that writing is born from the ache of contraries, polar-
ities in search of peace, of unity. But not the unity of making
mush. You want to live in the country. Your husband is an
urban boy. You compromise and both live in the suburbs. What
a squash of desire and energy.

Can you instead hold the tension until something fresh and
howling results? You must find your way to this when you
write.

Go ahead. Ten minutes. What bold restless extremes do you
carry inside? Write.

Scratch

Write about a time you itched. It could be physical or metaphor-
ical. Go. Ten minutes.

Sideways Step

To hammer home this idea of not entering your memoir head-on but coming upon a sidewards step, some structure or subject outside yourself to hang your memories on, think of one, two, five subjects that interest you and begin to write about them.

You pick gardening and you quit after writing about one rose you planted. Go a little further. How old were you? Whose house? What season? Give me the exact details. What did you think of while you dug the dirt? Dig deeper—was your mother sick then, who were you dating? Don't worry if this planting isn't your true entry point; it's practice. It'll fertilize the ghost behind you that's waiting to form—that ineffable cloud that will someday pour out of you.

Writing on this painter, that tire, the trees and rivers you love, all this creates space, attention, and time. If your dream is to become a great basketball player, playing marbles won't feed the dream. The same thing is true in writing. If you are looking for your true memoir material, don't dig up worms in the back-yard, dig in your notebook with a pen. That writing gets you aligned. The next day you trip over a rake on the sidewalk or have a weird glimpse of something as you teach algebra in front of the class and you realize that things are steering you in some direction. You need to stay in touch with notebook and pen, to be connected with the search. If you don't know you're looking, you won't find anything.

Rob Wilder taught workshops with me for four years. In his writing life he wrote fiction, good, well-crafted short stories, but they hadn't yet expressed his generosity, his crazy, ironic, smart-ass, dark humor and wit and his basic deep intelligence. In a sense, he was practicing writing, using the short story form. He wasn't conscious of this. He loved fiction. It was important to him and he made great effort in creating those stories. This effort honed his craft.

But writing has this quality where all the effort and desire in the world doesn't do shit. It's hard to comprehend. All our lives we've been taught to try hard. That's good, important to writing, too, but then in the middle of it, you have to be willing to jump off a hundred-foot pole with no net to catch you, no assurances. To let wind take you or the day or time or love. Writing's essential nature asks you not to go forward, not to be productive, not to be logical. In the middle of all your conservative striving, it asks you to take a step backward into the dark unknown—actually back into your real self, which has never been explored and you are not sure how to get there.

Eventually what you want is for your writing to become transparent. That your language and expression are not one iota off from who you are. A friend can read it and say, "Yup, that's Mary. Uh-huh, I'd know that voice anywhere—it's my old college friend Eddie." Does that mean if you are a girl from Brooklyn, you can't have a genuine character from Texas? Of course not, but if you have found genuine you, unhinged from your ideas about who "you" is, you can move more clearly and easily into a debutante, a Northeast accountant, a waitress from the Midwest, a cowboy—even into the head of the cowboy's horse.

When Rob and I taught together, I'd stand in front of sixty students and spontaneously call Rob up to the front. I thought I'd have a little fun.

"Rob," I'd say, "you have ten minutes, tell us how you became a writer. And I want you to talk for the full time."

He'd glare at me in disbelief, "I'm gonna kill you, Nat," but then you could see his mind working, whetted by the challenge. He'd launch into the story of working in advertising in New

York and at twenty-four leaving it all, driving across country in a beat-up bronze Ford station wagon, to write six hours a day in a run-down adobe in the Pecos, coming into Santa Fe at night to tend bar. It was a good story.

I asked him two other times in a year to tell that same story. Each time he filled in more details: how many notebooks he filled, the bread and cheese sandwiches he ate, the coyotes he encountered. A few students wept; they were all mesmerized. When he'd finished, I'd tap him on the shoulder, "Write it down."

He looked at me oddly. What was I talking about? A story about his life?—that's nothing to write about.

Sometimes I'd ask him, "Tell us about the teenagers you teach at Prep" or "Tell us about London—or Poppy." These are his two young children, whom he adores.

He began to feel more comfortable and the workshop attendees loved his stories. When he finished, I'd always nod, "Write it down." You could see his mind trying to make some leap—these ordinary stories?

Finally, he wrote one down—about his son London learning the word "pussy" and not knowing what it meant. To his surprise it was accepted immediately by *Salon,* an on-line magazine. An agent read it and contacted him. This sounds like all our fantasies, but Rob had worked hard for twenty years on his writing. Twenty years, a turn of the head, a sideways step, and that essay "Pussy" was produced.

Daddy Needs a Drink, irreverent essays about raising his two kids, has just come out. They are funny, mean, sarcastic, delightful—you can't stop reading. They are also intimate and tender. Vulnerable. This was true Rob, the way I knew him.

So now don't think—okay, I got it. I don't like kids, but I'm crazy about dogs. I'll write an essay about Elmer, my black Labrador—and the rest is history—publication, fame, movie rights, TV interviews. I've got to get a haircut and a new set of clothes.

It doesn't work that way. Remember? The sideways step. You can't hear Rob's story and try to copy it. That's another example of trying to grab your writing head-on.

You have to find your own set of coincidences. You make your own great—and crooked—path and at the same time be open for something to come to you. A meeting is involved—you and the large unknown. Let the mountains walk into your living room. Listen to the squawking yellow cabs. This is beginning to sound like a child's fantasy. You do need a child's mind. Something half innocent, and naïve, but also watchful, observant. Sophistication gets in the way, too complicated for finding your true home.

But remember: nothing lasts forever. That true home is not a solid edifice. A book may stay stationary on a table, but you are a moving work. You finish something, go on to the next.

Test III

I Remember

Two minutes on each of these topics:

____A memory of cabbage

____Some instance of a war

____A cup you loved

____A peace march you didn't attend

Monkey Mind

Where do thoughts come from, memories, words? All of it is carried in mind. Note: I didn't say "your mind" but "mind" itself because we are all run by the same principles of mind. We each have our individual details but the functioning of mind works the same way in all people.

You interrupt here to assure me that you are way more messed up than most minds. You won't fit, you can't write, you are hopeless.

Everyone feels this way. Shut up and listen. Yes, you are special but your mind isn't. Your mind at its base functions like all other human minds, just as your legs walk similarly to other people's and your hands do the same gripping and touching, poking and holding.

One basic thing the mind does is generate thoughts. The problem is: it's hard to settle it down. The mind has a tendency to wander and drift off or barrage us. Even before we get to a first thought—the ones that carry vitality, that are connected to the body—we are lost in critical second and third thoughts: "I can't do this writing. There's a sale on tuna. My kids need attention. I have nothing to say. I'm boring." These divisive, churning thoughts are telling you a lot, but not what they are actually saying. It's an indication of nervousness and energy. It tells you you want writing bad, but at the same time are terrified to write.

We call this monkey mind or the critic or editor. We run from this voice, but at the same time we believe it, listen to it as though it were God declaring the sacred truth: yes, indeed, you are a dud. And don't try to be anybody. Don't speak.

Everyone has this voice. Even if you had the ultimate in supportive parents and encouraging teachers, the human mind generates this old survival technique. Can you imagine if cave people had decided to wander off and contemplate their past? They wouldn't have gotten meat on the table. But this inheritance is not obsolete. We still have a fear of our inner world. Will we survive if we take time to think, to examine, to understand? Instead we prefer to go hurtling from one war to another, from one marriage to another, from one painful situation smack-dab into one more. We think that if we stay blind, ignorant, and keep going, we will make it through.

And plop!—in the middle of all this you decide you want to write a memoir, to look back, to ponder. Of course, your deep survival mechanism, old monkey mind, is going to go bananas.

It wants to protect you at all costs. But it's also testing you. Do you have the mettle, the wherewithal, to behold the gems of your heart? The jewels are sometimes handed to you bleeding, encased in betrayal and deception, reeking of disappointment and disillusion, slimy with heartbreak and pain. How bad do you want the bright pearls?

This is important for you to understand. It helps you to bear up under the screeching in your ear. Monkey mind can take the form of your mother, a nun, a professor, a priest—whatever it needs in order to do the job.

Your job, in the middle of this noise, is to keep your hand moving, to be steadfast. Find people to do timed writings with you, make a schedule even if it's only twice a week for half an hour—and stay with that schedule. (Be realistic. If you can only write once in the coming week, put it on your calendar. And show up. You don't blithely cancel a doctor's appointment—this date is as important.) Do what it takes.

With time and determination—sometimes a lot of determination—monkey mind does quiet down, does settle. It never goes away, but you create a genuine understanding of it. It will never so easily run your life again. At the same time, you are developing a curiosity, a commitment, and a love of the writing process. You are following what pleases you. Monkey mind's screeching can't get as much attention.

Eventually monkey mind's concern with survival transforms. You finally hold the jewels. You rule now. Monkey mind becomes the guardian at your gate. She's not a squawker anymore. She pays silent vigil, has joined your forces. But you won't recognize her right away. Your armor now is compassion, your defense, love. The jewels are in your hands. No one else's.

Wild at Heart

In the essay "Wild at Heart" in a book called *The Poem That Changed America: "Howl" Fifty Years Later,* Vivian Gornick writes:

> Allen Ginsberg was born in Newark, New Jersey, in 1926 to Louis and Naomi Ginsberg; the father was a published poet, a high school teacher, and a socialist; the mother, an enchanting free spirit, a passionate communist, and a woman who lost her mental stability in her thirties (ultimately she was placed in an institution and lobotomized). Allen and his brother grew up inside a chaotic mixture of striving respectability, left-wing bohemianism, and certifiable madness in the living room. It all felt *large* to the complicated, oversensitive boy who, discovering that he lusted after boys, began to feel mad himself and, like his paranoid parents, threatened by, yet defiant of, the America beyond the front door.
>
> None of this accounts for Allen Ginsberg; it only describes the raw material that, when the time was right, would convert into a poetic vision of mythic proportion that merged brilliantly with its moment: the complicated aftermath of the Second World War . . .

Let's look at this. The first paragraph is a detailed list of the specifics of Allen Ginsberg's early life. Yes, he was born in Newark; yes, yes, his father was what Gornick says he was and his mother is described aptly. It is true he was inclined to love boys when he was young. But then the stunning line: "None of

59

this accounts for Allen Ginsberg." Huh? I thought in writing we build up the details and create a picture of who we are? This is exactly the problematic trick.

You can be told what materials make a hand—the skin, the fine bones, the nails, the persnickety thumb, but then all the ingredients fuse and explode. Whose hand is this? A leap happens. Allen Ginsberg became a huge figure that changed the face of poetry. Notice, too, it is not only Allen Ginsberg the man, who created himself, but also his work that met the moment— he ignited with his time. Something dynamic happened.

We don't live in a vacuum. That extra ingredient—the flint snapping across the rough edge of our era, the day the news broke, the flavor of our decade, our generation—makes the spark spring up. You never talk just for yourself. A whole flame shoots through you. Even if you're not aware of it, even though your sorrow, your pain is individual, it is also connected to the large river of suffering. When you join the two, something materializes.

When Bob Dylan sat in the third row first seat in B. J. Rolfzen's English class in Hibbing High School, this public school teacher had no idea that this quiet boy would, two years after he left his family at eighteen, write some of the best songs of the twentieth century.

Allen Ginsberg and Bob Dylan were brought up thousands of miles apart. Bob Dylan had stable middle-class parents. His father sold electrical equipment, stoves, refrigerators to iron ore miners in Northern Minnesota. His mother belonged to B'nai B'rith. But "none of this accounts for" Bob Dylan. Dylan took a leap into another life. As an adult fourteen years older than Bob Dylan, Allen Ginsberg heard Dylan's songs and knew the torch of inspiration, of freedom, had been passed on to the next generation.

We each are endowed with original mind, which is like a river under the visible river, unconditioned, the immediate point where our clear consciousness meets the vast unknown; yet we've blown smoke screens to cloud it. Fake images, false illusions. When Allen Ginsberg sat down one night in his twenties to write what was really on his mind, he replaced the rhymed poesy he'd learned from his father and from school. That decision was the beginning of one of the most famous poems in our language. Imagine! the power of writing what's truly on your mind. What you really see, think, and feel. Rather than what you are told you should think, see, and feel. It causes a revolution— or at the very least, a damn fine poem.

Raw material is poured into a burning vat and something different comes out. Maybe in past generations when people didn't leave home and raised their children near their parents in the same town where they grew up and if your father was a steelworker, you became a steelworker or if your mother was a secretary, you became an office manager, you might not have had the luxury of wondering about yourself. You might not ponder how A became B and produced C. It might all have been obvious. But I bet that even a third-generation physician on his way to work in his hometown who suddenly notices the glint off a parking meter, stops still and questions: Who am I? and is left in this swirl that doesn't make sense. One lives and then one dies? Who thought this scheme up anyway?

We go back to our past to piece things together. "I always loved coffee ice cream, roast beef, and hopscotch." It still makes us happy to remember these things, but how did they lead to moving from the sprawl of a city on the East Coast to listening to mourning doves on a dead branch outside our kitchen door in the vast West? Can we turn around fast enough to catch a glimpse of our own face?

In some ways writing is our attempt to grasp what went on. We want an answer. We want things to be black and white, to be obvious and ordered. Oh, the relief. But have you noticed, it doesn't work that way? We live more in the mix of black and white, in the gray—or in the brilliant colors of the undefined moment.

Can we bear to hang out in incongruity, in that big word, paradox? How did I end up with the partner I have, the children that sprang from me? How can I love my father, who betrayed me? This isn't a call to ditch it all even though nothing makes sense. Instead, don't reject anything—the person who did something unforgivable, the white rose at the edge of your driveway, the split pea soup you never liked.

There are no great answers for who we are. Don't wait for them. Pick up the pen and right now in ten furious minutes tell the story of your life. I'm not kidding. Ten minutes of continuous writing is much more expedient than ten years of musing and getting nowhere.

Include the false starts, the wrong turns, the one surprising right thing that happened. A lot of it is ungrabbable—but you might sense an aroma, a whiff of something. Always in writing at the back of words are no words, behind you is nothing. That nothing holds us up. Embrace it.

In 1997 at the age of seventy, Allen Ginsberg heard from his doctor that he only had a short time to live, and he cried. Then sitting in his hospital bed he picked up a pen and worked on a poem he was writing. That man had an abundant heart. His death was important, but so was a poem. Soon before the end he stayed up into the morning hours, making long distance calls to friends to say good-bye, to ask if they needed anything, were they taken care of, should he leave them funds in his will.

I tell you all this because there is a sea of possibility out there. Again, I say pick up the pen and find it for yourself. Don't begin with an idea: Begin to understand your life—and death—with the point of the pen touching paper.

Allen Ginsberg

I studied with Allen Ginsberg in 1976 at the Jack Kerouac School of Disembodied Poetics. It was a six-week summer course in Boulder, Colorado. I was twenty-eight years old and the path of my life was set, even though I didn't fully know it. About fifteen years later I had the privilege of teaching with him in L.A. And the following year I taught a weekend course and forum with him again for Pacifica College in the same auditorium in L.A. There were six hundred students.

We each taught half the room and then switched. I gave a talk about practice. He read his poems. On the last morning we had breakfast together in the hotel. He ordered only low cholesterol food. He said it was his doctor's orders.

I called my friend Barbara Schmitz, who I had met in his class so many years before. "Imagine," I said, "I'm teaching with Allen Ginsberg."

"Don't you remember what you said back then? 'He doesn't recognize me now, but some day he will.'"

"I said that?"

"Uh huh."

He has been dead for nine years and I miss him. Whenever I lead a retreat I put on the altar a yellow-framed photo of him sitting cross-legged in meditation position. He is wearing a sly little smile on his face. Right in the middle of effort, don't be serious, he seems to be saying—or who are we anyway? he asks. Many of my students don't seem to know what to make of

Allen Ginsberg. Some think that he looks like an old man. And some recall rumors of his sexual escapades.

He used to sing accompanied with his harmonium a song he'd written called "Gospel Noble Truths": "Sit when you sit; talk when you talk; cry when you cry; lie down when you lie down and die when you die." He'd repeat the phrase "die when you die" several times at the end in a wavery voice. He wasn't a good singer, but the students liked hearing him. His voice was so sincere. It gave you courage and made you want to step up and sing too.

The leaves were so green that summer in Boulder when I first studied with him. When I was alone I'd sing his song at the top of my lungs in my own crooked voice. He was one of my most important teachers.

All over again I want to honor him. After a long walk up the side of a mountain, I want to reach back one more time into the same dark past I wrote about before to say thank you again, you are in the lineage of my fifty-eight years.

It is our hope that writing releases us. Instead maybe it deepens the echo. We call out to our past and the call comes back. We are alone—and not alone.

Plain

Tell me about someone who was a true teacher for you. Don't be sentimental. Tell it straight and plain: who was this person? Go. Ten minutes.

Bolt

Tell me about a time something dawned on you, a realization, worlds came together or simply you saw a lightning bolt on a mountain. Where were you? Go for ten minutes.

Bicycle

Tell me a memory associated with a bicycle. The spokes, the wheels, the narrow seat. Go for ten.

Great Students

Often we remember a great teacher: we've heard about the English teacher in high school "who saved my life," the history teacher "who gave me direction," or the spiritual teacher "who opened my heart." But what about great students we knew? The one in physical education class who made so much effort, the one in math class who chewed her pencil to a stub. Write about great students you remember. Maybe you were even one of them at one time in your life. Remember them not because they got an A but because of their earnest effort, their lousy handwriting, their inability to do anything right.

Don't limit students to people you knew at school. How about at work, at church, in your Zen practice? Let's honor them now. Go ten minutes. Go twenty minutes. Take as much time as you need.

This is an example of bringing out what you have not noticed, of focusing on the negative space, not the tree but what is around the tree. You're focusing not on the teacher but the key element that creates the teacher. No teacher exists without students.

Moment

In 1977 on Morada Lane in a small adobe behind a coyote fence I taught the first writing practice group to eight Taos women. For the last twenty years I have taught these same workshops at the Mabel Dodge Luhan House a few hundred yards farther up on Morada Lane. I joke: I have not gone a very far distance in my life.

Students come and go. Eventually we all will die. I fear I will have forgotten to die. I'll be standing in front of the class after everyone I know has long passed.

"Class, get out your pens."

Please help me. If all of you write right now, maybe I can let go and die too. My job will be complete.

We talk about eternity. I'm afraid sometimes the only thing that will continue is our incessant, chattering thoughts. After all, monkey mind keeps going at the same time we are making love, driving, walking, eating, playing tennis, writing. It takes notice of nothing. It just keeps on. Have you noticed? Yada, yada, yada. Why should our dying be any different? Our wandering thoughts won't pay any attention, but will keep on going like a full set of dental impressions, mouthing their way into the afterlife.

See if you can nail down eternity right now. Give me this sterling moment, just as it is. Don't run out and buy a new dress and a pair of stunning sunglasses. This is it: just as you are. Get it down. Go.

Now move from this present moment. Jot down other

moments you remember, that were strong and clear for you. They don't have to be momentous—such as when you won the State Bowling Championship or said "I do" at the altar. The mind doesn't work that way. Often it recalls some odd sniggley instance: you bought a box of oil pastels at a sidewalk sale in some suburb outside Philadelphia or the time you were frightened of a tailgater you spotted glugging down a beer, his car parked under a bridge waiting for a November Steelers' game in Pittsburgh. Or the taste of metal when the water ran off a rusty pipe early one summer morning in Northern Minnesota; the lilac tree you came upon one May in Santa Fe when you turned the corner. You thought of your mother. She once loved lilacs. You stepped up to the bush and touched the blossoms. A shiver ran through you. Right down into the marrow you knew you would have to live out one by one the interminable last days of your mother's life.

Notice that I first asked you to give me the present moment. The present grounds the mind. Look over your shoulder. No past over there. The past can only be found in the present when it comes alive in you. Remember: only you carry that past. You bring it into focus now.

You find yourself suddenly crying. That's fine. Just as long as you keep writing. Don't stop the hand. Write through your emotions. On to another moment. This time you are laughing. Great. Feel what you feel. But don't be thrown off balance and drop your pen. You began with writing. Finish with it. Writing is your practice as you mow through your memories, the even chord among the highs and lows.

Feel how fluid the mind can be. Moving your pen helps to keep things from getting snagged, caught on some old branch of thought and not being able to go on.

Zora Neale Hurston

Feeling a little whacko? Good. That's sometimes the intention of writing practice. Only when you break down your usual way of thinking—the convenient, comfortable, easy, polite response—will you touch the textured grain of your life. You will need to crack open structure: scramble up the neat rows of chairs, the well-lined pile of towels and notebooks. Submerge yourself below the standard version of the way your mother, father, school want you to remember your childhood to the way it really was for you. If you were miserable, say it. If you hated peas and those white cardboard containers of milk, put that down. If you had a crush on your Spanish teacher and it was the only reason you mustered an A, claim that love right now.

Feeling crazy might not be bad. It might be the disintegration of the not-true world you tried to maintain. Maybe you'll find that you were wonderful after all but believed your brother's image of you instead. You weren't a dummy for loving Shakespeare and Keats. You just were different.

The following excerpt was written by Zora Neale Hurston, an African American writer, whose works include *Their Eyes Were Watching God* and *Dust Tracks on a Road*. She was born in Florida in 1891 and died in the same state in 1960.

> I remember the very day that I became colored. Up to my thirteenth year I lived in the little negro town of Eatonville, Florida. It is exclusively a colored town. The only white people I knew passed through the town going to or coming from Orlando.

The native whites rode dusty horses, the Northern tourists chugged down the sandy village road in automobiles. The town knew the Southerners and never stopped cane chewing when they passed. But the Northerners were something else again. They were peered at cautiously from behind curtains by the timid. The more venturesome would come out on the porch to watch them go past and got just as much pleasure out of the tourists as the tourists got out of the village.

The front porch might seem a daring place for the rest of the town, but it was a gallery seat for me. My favorite place was atop the gate-post. Proscenium box for a born first-nighter. Not only did I enjoy the show, but I didn't mind the actors knowing that I liked it. I usually spoke to them in passing. I'd wave at them and when they returned my salute, I would say something like this: "Howdy-do-well-I-thank-you-where-you-goin'?" Usually automobile or the horse paused at this, and after a queer exchange of compliments, I would probably "go a piece of the way" with them, as we say in farthest Florida. If one of my family happened to come to the front in time to see me, of course negotiations would be rudely broken off. But even so, it is clear that I was the first "welcome-to-our-state" Floridian, and I hope the Miami Chamber of Commerce will please take notice.

During this period, white people differed from colored to me only in that they rode through town and never lived there. They liked to hear me "speak pieces" and sing and wanted to see me dance the parse-me-la, and gave me generously of their small silver for doing these things, which seemed strange to me for I wanted to do them so much that I needed bribing to stop. Only they didn't know it. The colored people gave no dimes. They deplored any joyful tendencies in me, but I was their Zora nevertheless. I belonged to them, to the nearby hotels, to the county—everybody's Zora.

But changes came in the family when I was thirteen, and I was sent to school in Jacksonville. I left Eatonville, the town of

the oleanders, as Zora. When I disembarked from the river-
boat at Jacksonville, she was no more. It seemed that I had suffered a sea change. I was not Zora of Orange County any more,
I was now a little colored girl. I found it out in certain ways.
In my heart as well as in the mirror, I became a fast brown—
warranted not to rub nor run.

—from *How It Feels to Be Colored Me*

This was written in 1928. It is clear Hurston trusted her
own mind and wrote from experience.

List thirty ways you felt different from others as a child.

Now write a full ten minutes about one time you didn't fit
in, whether it was because of race, religion, sexual preference,
the shape of your body, your black toenail, your dark mind. You
name it and write about it. We all have these experiences. It's
odd how we are supposed to be cool, smooth as butter, act as
though there is no place in which we weren't accepted or hurt.
How ridiculous. This is a tough world. This is your memoir.
Get real about your life.

Reading Aloud

It's a good idea from time to time to read aloud things you've written. When we write, often we don't know what we have said, because as we move the hand across the page, we are paying attention to monkey mind, that critic always at our ear that rants on how we shouldn't write, and who do we think we are? This voice is so loud that when we stop writing, we have no way to gain access to what we have actually written. All we have heard is the criticism. We feel like shit. This tends to build and fester. Reading aloud releases the tension, allows you to connect with what you actually wrote. No good or bad. You can go on.

Why don't you arbitrarily open to any page in your notebook and find someone to read it to.

Tell your friend you want to hear what you've written by reading it aloud to her, that you don't need her comments. That will relax her. For some reason any time someone hears writing, they think they have to become the *New York Times* critic of the year. Or they have to be nice—and encouraging. "I think it was lovely, just lovely, that you peed in your pants till you were twelve." Tell them to be quiet and listen. That's all you want.

But why can't I line up the toaster, the blender, the microwave in the kitchen and read to them? you ask.

Reading to another human being is more naked than reciting to the wall. You are more exposed, can't hide anymore. Get used to it. It makes your memoir alive. It closes the gap between what you believed you wrote and what you really wrote. It allows you to hear yourself, mirrored back from the silent mind of the listener.

If your friend is bursting, ask her for a *recall*—anything she can remember, staying as close as she can to what you read. You don't want analysis: "Your writing was about justice." You want reflection: "Abigail rode through the plum orchard."

If she just remembers singular words, that's fine: branch, fist, horse. *Recall* gives your listeners an activity for their nervous energy, but it also gives you feedback—what was strong and remembered. This reflection makes you notice something you might not have noticed on your own about your writing. "The bent garbage can," someone recalls. That small detail matters. Here is reinforcement to continue to note the odd particular or exact, quiet element—the "ironed" napkin, "rough" pebble, "crumpled" peony by the side of the road. It also lets you know someone was there. You are not alone.

Sitting

Sitting meditation is something you might want to try. It is a way to come into closer intimacy with your mind. What really are a writer's tools? Pen, paper, and the human mind. The more we understand the mind, the better we can use this tool. In sitting there is nothing in between you and a direct meeting with your thoughts, the emptiness around them, the room you are in, the light, your breath, your belly grumbling. Even pen and paper are put aside.

Sit in a chair or cross-legged on a cushion. Settle in comfortably and be with yourself. Anchor your mind by feeling the breath going in and out at your nose or feeling your belly or chest rise and fall.

You "anchor" the mind with your pen when you write. So in sitting you do it with your breath. An untethered boat will drift on the waves and pretty soon be gone over the horizon. This is true about your mind, too. You can get lost in discursive thinking, unless you anchor yourself, give your mind ground to come back to.

Close your eyes or keep them at a forty-five degree angle unfocused. You might want to take off your glasses.

Every time your mind wanders bring it back to the breath.

The idea isn't to glue your mind and your breath together. The real practice is to accept the mind; if it gets distracted, bring it gently back. As many times as it wanders, redirect its attention to your breath.

This returning to the breath is a reminder: yoo-hoo, here you are. You are not twenty years ago in the stacks at the university library or climbing Mount Everest or purchasing a red see-through blouse right now. You are here, breathing. The carpet is maroon, the walls, a pale yellow. A wren twitters outside.

But how can I go into my memoir if I'm here, present only in this moment?

If you are present now, the past becomes clearer, more precise. You know who you are—then what you were.

When you are present you have more resources to call on. If I take a bite of toast now, I might suddenly remember that nip I took of her shoulder ten years ago in the hotel and understand how that next kiss flung me into a long crazy wrong love affair. You begin to see how interconnected instances, moments, situations, human beings are. Isn't that what memoir is? Not a straitjacket of experience where we file away each event, memoir instead rolls through our mind in a long circuitous route like a bright, pink ribbon. Nothing rigid about it. It includes the breath, this in and out of air, taking in and giving out.

It is a misunderstanding to think that sitting with your breath zones you out, makes you so tranquil you can't lift a pen. Sitting stirs the red hot coals. You might discover you are hungry, you are angry, you have been spaced-out. But at least sitting presents these things to you, serves them up on a plate. It's unbearable, but it's part of you.

Sit for ten minutes. Then write for ten like a mad hatter, a sorcerer, a person whose hair is on fire. Tell us, what is this life you have been living? Go. Ten minutes.

Hand

Here is a variation on sitting: instead of returning to your breath, you might try anchoring your mind in the feeling of your hands. You might have them palm up or palm down on your knees or resting on your thighs or clasped in front of you. The mind wanders; come back to the feeling of your hands. The mind wanders; come back to the hands.

But, you say, I've been anchoring with the breath for three weeks. When I just now switched to the hands instead of the breath, suddenly the breath has gotten more of my attention.

Well, isn't that good? Before, when the breath was your anchor, your thoughts got your attention. This time the hands brought you to your breath. You can make your contrary nature work for yourself.

Play with it. See what helps and what doesn't. None of this is carved in stone. Try anchoring in the feeling of your two lips together or, if you are sitting in a chair, your two feet touching the floor.

The important thing is to keep this sitting practice alive. It's not an opportunity to zone out. Be curious, playful. Stay in there with it. How best can you learn to be right here?

Hearing

On the whole, writers are an auditory group. They have a natural inclination to listen, not only to what people say, but they take in what's around the words—the shadows, the curtains, what's not being said. They also listen to their own minds, to unlikely insights, odd intuitions, thoughts, sentences, inner and outer rhythms.

For this reason, try using sound to anchor the mind in sitting practice. Every time your mind wanders, come back to your ears and what they hear. If it's completely silent for a period of time when you are sitting, receive the silence. Don't reach for noise. On its own, the sound of a car's engine will arise, a bird will cheep, a door will slam, someone in another room will moan, a phone will ring, rain will hit the roof, a baby will cry. But don't hold onto the varied whimpers, roars, clacks, blasts, bangs, hubbubs, peals, tinkles, and blares. Let each sound appear and disappear, rise and fall. You are a living ear receiving sound and receiving silence.

Try it. Ten minutes.

One of my favorite Japanese poets, Ikkyu, became totally enlightened when he heard the sound of a crow overhead one midnight while he was meditating in his rowboat on Lake Biwa. As a poet Ikkyu had been attuning himself to the sound and melody of words. His ears were awake and alert. Caw Caw Caw—and the whole brilliant world illuminated his body.

What sound set your life spinning? Go. Write for ten minutes. Then sit and anchor your mind with sound for ten.

Chin

Try this: If your mind wanders a lot while you sit, tuck in your chin. That physical adjustment helps. Our head is usually way ahead of us, filled with thoughts. Rein it in.

Also sit up straighter. Get that spine to support you.

Another thing: sitting with open palms on your knees or thighs is an open hearted gesture but sometimes you want to pull in the energy and concentrate more. Put your hands together in what is called a mudra: right hand below left with thumb tips touching, creating a circle, held in front of your stomach.

This is a position of determination. Yes, you are saying, I will continually return to my anchor, no matter how much the mind drifts off.

What is the equivalent of this mudra in writing? A commitment that you will complete what you are working on. You will figure out how to do it, how to communicate what you have to say. You will do what it takes, no matter how long. You will not get discouraged. You will not undermine yourself. You will ask for help.

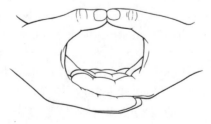

Tongue

Put the tip of your tongue behind your upper front teeth when you are sitting. This keeps the jaw from tensing.

The different positions of the body help to hold the mind in equilibrium.

Practicing writing regularly calms the mind, not because you write about nice things, but because your fears, anxieties, your troubled thoughts know they will have a place and time to express themselves.

Slowly in this way you will build the story of your life. You will figure out how to form your memoir. You will record your experience—all of it, the details and the felt truths below the circumstances.

Just Sitting—or Do the Neola

Okay, while we are on a roll, let's try something else, too. Drop it all—forget about the breath, hands, ears, chin. Throw the anchor out the window or into the center of the Indian Ocean.

Now let's just sit for twenty minutes. Don't worry if fifteen of the twenty are spent obsessing about your wedding dress and it turns out you're sixty and in all likelihood you won't marry again. Or you drifted off to a deep desire to suddenly cut your toenails, and you thought about it over and over—where you would get the clippers, how you'd bend over the tub rim. Oh, such fine detail.

For the first few years every retreat I sat I imagined making a pot roast. I'd carefully peel the onions, get out the cutting board. Add carrots, brown the meat. It made no sense. I never cooked one when the retreat was over—or thought about it in my daily life.

This is the mind. If you were only present to the sitting for a moment in the full twenty minutes, you did not fail. There is no success or failure, no great place you are going. You are "just sitting." To wander, to obsess, to lust—you get a flavor of the mind, a direct meeting. Without acting on any of the thoughts, you get to see how they rise up and—if you're lucky—pass away. Sometimes we get stuck. You get to observe the nature of being stuck.

But eventually with this "just sitting," thoughts are just another thing, like snow out the window. They get your attention for a moment and then they don't. We need to give enough space in "just sitting" for our thoughts to settle. Let the mind quiet of its own accord. It takes time to become who we are.

It's like shaking up vinegar and oil. Put down the bottle and wait for the vinegar to sink to the bottom, for the oil to become clear. Sit still and watch it happen inside you.

In "just sitting" you can drop any exact effort. There is a sound. You hear the sound. You feel hands on thighs. Then you might notice your breathe. Finally you are propelled into the deep unknown: open space between sound or feeling or the vagaries of your thoughts. Just here.

I'd been taught just sitting in a very formal way, but it didn't become mine until thirty years later when it seemed I gave up everything for a few months. Daily I went to a café called Bread and Chocolate and sat at a table near a big window, holding onto a tall cup of steaming water, taking an occasional sip and nibbling at a chocolate chip cookie that had to last an hour. It was then I dropped all effort, even discursive thinking came and went. I wasn't caught by anything.

Maybe it was all the practice before that brought me to this place. Maybe I was finally exhausted. But you don't need thirty years to discover it.

I have a student named Neola. Isn't that a fine name? When I first met her, I immediately started a little ditty: Roll over, Mineola . . .

When nothing else seemed to work for her I suggested she go to a café and "just sit." I created a shorthand for "just sitting": "Do the Neola," I told the class.

Neola loved having something named after her. And when a practice is your namesake you have to get good at it. I told her to write me a postcard from one of the cafés. Then I gave her another instruction to confound her—always follow the person behind you.

Ridiculous? No? Yes? You figure it out. Don't exclude anything, including the dog bark, dozen roses and daylilies, the wails in Iraq, the cement, the nothing that was your life. Being right on the point, the point being there is no point. You go out between breaths. Your notebook becomes luminous. You suddenly know what to write.

One of the students said, "'Do the Neola' sounds like a dance."

Yes. A dance. The great dance.

Practice Notebook

You might want to have a small separate notebook where you note your sitting practice. Record the date, where you sat, how long, and a few lines of commentary. For example:

> July 6, sat 4:30–4:50 in afternoon on green couch in living room, couldn't concentrate. Worried about my job.
> July 7, skipped.
> July 8, sat 6:00 am for 30 minutes, planned to sit 20 but felt so good I kept going. Didn't sleep well and the sitting seemed to save me.

It's important to record the days you skipped, because then you are facing, accepting, and including them, too. They don't need to be blank spaces you are ashamed of or feel guilty about or haunted by. Instead of neglecting them, you are also aware of them.

And be realistic: don't set yourself up and say I will sit every day. It will then become like giving up alcohol. You blow it with a beer one night and never find your way out of a bar. Maybe sitting five times a week is realistic for you. Maybe four times for ten minutes each time is what you need to set up.

In addition to your sitting practice notebook, you might also want to have a separate writing practice notebook to jot down the date and whether you wrote, where, how long, about what?

Let's say that you don't write for a week, two weeks. You still are obligated to note the date and write in "skipped." You don't need to write the excuse. This act of noting makes your writing—or not writing—conscious. It plants a seed; you stay connected.

Walking

May I suggest one more practice? Walking.

Often we run ahead of ourselves and dash about. When we walk slowly we have a chance to let the world come home to us. There is no place we are going; no place we have to get to. We are just walking, placing one foot down after the other. What a privilege it is to have feet and legs, knees and hips. Not everyone does, you know.

With writing we anchor the mind with the pen; with sitting, the breath; with walking we anchor our mind with the bottoms of our feet.

Notice how you prepare to take the next step. A shift of weight, one foot in the air before it lands on solid ground. Don't be stiff or self-conscious. Relax and take one slow step. Feel the sole of your foot. Let your arms hang at your sides—or if you need to, clasp them at your back or front.

You can look around, but not with a grasping mind: Ohh, I like that dress in the window. I want it. Or that tree—what's its name? I should plant one in my front yard. Instead see color, the texture of bark. Without commentary receive what you see through your eyes. If looking is too distracting, and it might be in the beginning, walk with your eyes down at a forty-five-degree angle.

This kind of walking brings much peace and happiness. I work hard to try to convey the true experience of it to my students. This grounding in the act of walking creates a feeling of possibility and confidence.

Five years ago at a writing workshop in Manhattan, I assigned the students to do slow walking for a half hour during their lunch break. I did it, too. I marveled at how much more I noticed the city around me. The bricks alone on buildings were a wonder.

Fifteen minutes into it a large man ran up and hovered. "Where's the bus going downtown?" he screamed frantically into my face.

I looked up—we were also supposed to walk in silence—and I shrugged, shook my head, and turned up my palms. I had no idea which bus to take.

He stared at me. "You don't know shit," he spat out and ran off.

He was right. I smiled. I took my next step. I had nothing to defend when I walked like this.

Another time I cajoled a group of eighty writing students to do slow walking in Washington Square Park. Most of them were New Yorkers. They thought I was nuts.

We could get killed, they said.

Surprisingly the square was almost empty. The Gay Pride Parade was passing on the other side of the square. Everyone had gone over there to gawk. There was loud music, cheers, floats, and costumes. We stepped in silence, one foot after the other. All at once it was quiet. Everyone on the other side of the square had stopped and was staring at us, including the people in costumes on floats. Silence and slowness was such an unusual act that it even stopped a parade.

Linda Gregg

Here is a poem by Linda Gregg:

ARRIVING AGAIN AND AGAIN WITHOUT NOTICING

> I remember all the different kinds of years.
> Angry, or brokenhearted, or afraid.
> I remember feeling like that
> walking up the mountain along the dirt path
> to my broken house on the island.
> And long years of waiting in Massachusetts.
> The winter walking and hot summer walking.
> I finally fell in love with all of it:
> dirt, night, rock and far views.
> It's strange that my heart is as full
> now as my desire was then.

Look how she begins: *I remember,* using what we are practicing for memoir. We don't know all the details of her life but in a few lines we get the feeling arc and transformation of her years. Poetry is a rare duck. Don't think a poet doesn't sweat and suffer—but then they produce a gem with a few strokes that seem to make life seamless. Read this poem again (and again). She walks, she remembers. This is what I've been talking about. I won't explain further. You don't need to understand right now. You only need to practice writing and walking and the flower of your experience will burn forth—a true memoir.

Happy

Without thinking, trusting the first thing your mind flashes on, tell me what was the happiest time in your life. You think: sitting on the curb, eight years old, watching two ants fight. You think: Being in love with the wrong person. He was in the kitchen with you. You were talking about cats. Your wife was in the next room. You think: Biting into an orange. Age twenty-four. Cambridge, Mass. A bookstore was across the street.

You have ten minutes now to write. See where your first flash leads you. You can go far in ten minutes, smack into something you never understood before—and now you have it. At least for this writing. Everything slips through the hand like quicksilver. But go. Get down as much as you can. Ten minutes can fill the universe: The happiest time in your life.

Ice Cream

Tell me everything you know about ice cream. Go.
Ten minutes.

Cook

Deborah Madison, a wonderful cook, lives in Galisteo, New Mexico, a twenty-five-minute drive from Santa Fe, past the Lamy train station, where passengers from Chicago, tired and dusty from their long trip, step off the express and behold big skies, sage and piñon, arroyos, jagged red earth in dry country.

Deborah has published many fine cookbooks, most recently one on vegetarian soups, which I'd meant to pick up at the local bookstore. I own several of her other classics, *The Savory Way, The Greens Cookbook,* but writers love attention for their latest publication. I know this and wanted to bring it to her to sign when I went there for lunch. Instead I had in hand a slice of watermelon soap. It was a mauve color and smelled like— you guessed it—the fat fruit. But not a cloying smell. Just right for a cook, I hoped.

We had what Deborah called a ragout for lunch, fresh green vegetables simmered in a mushroom broth with dumplings floating in the bowl.

I liked the fresh strawberries in cream we were eating for dessert. She corrected me, "They were first poached in wine."

"Of course," I said.

"It's called a berry fool." I had her spell "fool" for me. "You can have any kind of fruit fool."

I am a fool for this fool, I thought.

She is in the process of creating a dessert cookbook. She served a large meringue with the fool. She said it didn't come out quite right, too brown. I gobbled it up. She also had a galette wrapped in a bag. She cut two slices.

I was in heaven.

It's rare to find a person who doesn't like to eat. Because so many of our senses are involved at the same time—taste, smell, seeing, feeling—we are charged up when we eat. Often we eat unconsciously, unaware, but the senses are noting just the same. We have only to go back in our minds and recall.

Write ten minutes: when did you taste your favorite fruit for the first time? You don't remember? Imagine it. This is a way to recharge your memory and not feel on the spot to dish out the exact details immediately. Imagining often leads to the real deal—that apricot hanging from a tree. Tasting a fruit for the first time might not mean the first time that berry ever entered your mouth, but the first time you actually were present and noticed. The first time you wake up to cherries might be when you write about it.

One more ten minutes: Give me a recipe you love. It could be as simple as a glass of milk. How did you discover that fine beverage? What kind of glass do you serve it in? Where did the milk come from? Go.

Potatoes

Ten minutes:
Write everything you know about mashed potatoes.

Verb

Make your verbs alive. They carry the energy of a sentence. Check your use of "to be." Can you use another, more dynamic verb instead? "I *was* on my bike and rode to the store." How about, "I *pedaled* my bike to the grocer." You can feel the pumping going on. Fewer words, even more economical.

Here's a list of alternative verbs for the verb "to bless":

consecrate
sanctify
permit
allow
honor
praise
dedicate
exalt
glorify
hallow

But that does not mean never use "bless." Sometimes "bless" is right on the mark and no other word will do. But let yourself be flexible, jaunty. Have alternate verbs in your pocket.

Take a single verb: to go. What other words can you use? You make a list.

Hard and Soft

This is a reminder: you have to be firm with monkey mind and aware of its shape shifting. One day it uses the tactic: *my writing is going nowhere. It's a useless activity.* And you quit. The next day you try again. Monkey mind also tries again: *my writing is going nowhere. It's a useless task.* But in the middle of the night you realized you should have persevered. When you hear the same tactic on the second day, you don't buy it. You keep writing. Pretty good. But it doesn't take long before you have another thought: your daughter is in third grade. Wouldn't it be a treat if you baked cookies and brought them in for the whole class for snack time. This is your only week off from work. Next week you can't do it.

You start to argue: This is also my only week to write. I have no sugar at home. It will take all day to bake cookies. I'll go buy them.

Already you are caught. Don't argue with monkey mind. Let its voice run through but don't fight with it.

You have to be firm. You committed to writing and that's what you are doing.

But what if it's right? you ask. What if my writing is useless and the cookies are important?

In the middle of writing you have no clear analysis. Let writing do writing. Later, much later, after you've written a bunch, you can evaluate. Don't do it in the middle of writing. If you do—any angle that cuts you off, diminishes you from the act—rest assured, that is monkey mind.

So you are being asked to be resolute and, at the same time, in the center, receptive, open, allowing all thoughts, all life to come through you as you write.

Even monkey mind arrives as a momentary thought—*I hate myself, this is shit, I'm dumb.* Write that thought down. Don't get deterred, throw it in the pot, but keep going. Not so much chatter. Just the physical act of doing it.

Fierce and tender. Ruthless and soft. There are candies like that: tough on the outside, yummy on the inside. There are lovers like that, too.

What I say here about writing pertains to all of life, but right now we want a memoir and this is what you have to do.

Having a friend to write with keeps you honest. Your friend has her hand moving, you have to, too. You want to go to the bathroom, but you wait till the time is up. Can you imagine two friends jogging and one takes a break to pee? I don't think it happens.

Can you imagine two nations coming together with the determination of making peace, vowing to let no obstruction get in the way? But, you say, politics are so complicated. So is the country of the human mind. It can be done.

Please, practice. Practicing hard and soft will be a great aid. You don't know when you will be called on to save the world. For now, begin by saving yourself.

More Than Ten Minutes

Why do we always write for ten minutes? you ask.

I want to write for fifteen, twenty, a half-hour, you say.

Ten minutes is a convenient starting point. It's a sprint. Feel free to ease into longer runs. But don't abandon that ten-minute hard-core pressurized feeling that you have to get it all down on two or three pages. There is something wildly exhilarating about that: gun to the head, writing for life and death in ten minutes.

But please, be my guest. Write about what you regret for fifteen minutes. Then a waitress you fell in love with for twenty. It's a shift in energy. Maybe not so much the bing bang of ten but an ease and a longer breath. For heaven's sake, you've just been granted five, then ten more minutes. When you are writing, that's a whole lifetime. Take advantage of it. Go.

Sprinting

Let's look at this idea of sprinting. In truth, ten minutes is a long sprint.

Do three-minute sprints with each one of these:

cantaloupe
cow
breast
window
urine
pillow
swimsuit
vanilla

It's good to get a list from someone else. You end up writing about things you wouldn't have thought of on your own. It stretches you. Write absolutely anything that comes to mind for each thing. Up from under, the crazier the better.

It's also good to make your own list of eight things to sprint about. Don't think. Anything that comes to mind, jot it down.

Then run for your life. Three minutes of writing on each. Go down the list. Don't discriminate.

Sprinting is giving the mind a workout, getting it limber and open. Move that hand, grease those ball bearings inside your head. Keep them rolling. Have you noticed? They get stuck easily. Your thoughts can crank to a stop, frozen on one thing.

This practice makes your mind fluid. A fluid mind, a river that runs, helps the whole body, the entire environment. Be an ecologist. This earth won't last otherwise.

Come on. Enough philosophizing. Get moving. Three minutes and three minutes and three minutes. Keep going.

Religion

What religion were you brought up with? Ten minutes. Go.

A student once wrote: *a priest was drawing a penis on the blackboard.* You see, you don't have to become cumbersome when religion is mentioned. Dive right into the essence of your experience. No explanation.

Jimmy Santiago Baca

Jimmy Santiago Baca is a fine, powerful poet who lives in Albuquerque, New Mexico. Here is something from his first memoir, *Working in the Dark.*

Two years passed. I was twenty now, and behind bars again. The federal marshals had failed to provide convincing evidence to extradite me to Arizona on a drug charge, but still I was being held. They had ninety days to prove I was guilty. The only evidence against me was that my girlfriend had been at the scene of the crime with my driver's license in her purse. They had to come up with something else. But there was nothing else. Eventually they negotiated a deal with the actual drug dealer, who took the stand against me. When the judge hit me with a million-dollar bail, I emptied my pockets on his booking desk: twenty-six cents.

One night in my third month in the county jail, I was mopping the floor in front of the booking desk. Some detectives had kneed an old drunk and handcuffed him to the booking bars. His shrill screams raked my nerves like a hacksaw on bone, the desperate protest of his dignity against their inhumanity. But the detectives just laughed as he tried to rise and kicked him to his knees. When they went to the bathroom to pee and the desk attendant walked to the file cabinet to pull the arrest record, I shot my arm through the bars, grabbed one of the attendant's university textbooks, and tucked it in my overalls. It was the only way I had of protesting.

It was late when I returned to my cell. Under my blanket I switched on a pen flashlight and opened the thick book at random, scanning the pages. I could hear the jailer making his rounds on the other tiers. The jangle of his keys and the sharp click of his boot heels intensified my solitude. Slowly I enunciated the words . . . p-o-n-d, ri-pple. It scared me that I had been reduced to this to find comfort. I always had thought reading a waste of time, that nothing could be gained by it. Only by action, by moving out into the world and confronting and challenging the obstacles, could one learn anything worth knowing.

Even as I tried to convince myself that I was merely curious, I became so absorbed in how the sounds created music in me and happiness, I forgot where I was. Memories began to quiver in me, glowing with a strange but familiar intimacy in which I found refuge. For a while, a deep sadness overcame me, as if I had chanced on a long-lost friend and mourned the years of separation. But soon the heartache of having missed so much of life, that had numbed me since I was a child, gave way, as if a grave illness lifted itself from me and I was cured, innocently believing in the beauty of life again. I stumblingly repeated the author's name as I fell asleep, saying it over and over in the dark: Words-worth, Words-worth.

Before long my sister came to visit me, and I joked about taking her to a place called Kubla Khan and getting her a blind date with this *vato* named Coleridge who lived on the seacoast and was *malias* on morphine. When I asked her to make a trip into enemy territory to buy me a grammar book, she said she couldn't. Bookstores intimidated her, because she, too, could neither read nor write.

Days later, with a stub pencil I whittled sharp with my teeth, I propped a Red Chief notebook on my knees and wrote my first words. From that moment, a hunger for poetry possessed me.

Baca's writing is visceral: click of boot heels, jangle of keys, stub pencil whittled with teeth, shrill screams, raked nerves, hacksaw on bone. His memories quiver and glow. Writing is a felt body experience for him. It physically moves—and changes—his life.

He wrote another memoir, *A Place to Stand,* where he tells in detail how he learned to write—and to study poetry—in maximum security prison. At one point he gets into a fight with another inmate and as he hovers over him about to plunge a blade into his heart, he hears in his head the words of Garcia Lorca and Pablo Neruda, two great Spanish poets he'd just been reading. How can you kill and still be a poet? he asks himself as he is torn between the tough, ruthless code of survival he learned in the streets and the cherishing of all earthly things he'd been absorbing in poetry. Finally he drops the shank. A bell goes off. The guards come. He survived killing someone. Poetry won out. A great victory for all of us.

Some people might hear this story of Baca's and, being perhaps selfish, nervous, or insecure, feel diminished by it rather than inspired. Maybe when you read it, you worried about your own memoir and you worry about yourself. I'm a pale, pudgy white girl. What can I write? I'm a comfortable, middle-class brown boy—I don't fit the stereotype. What value would my memoir be?

Do not use Baca's—or any other writer's—memoir as a deterrent, an opponent, a cause to belittle yourself. Instead be encouraged by his perseverance. If he can do it under those extreme circumstances you can quit complaining and bemoaning your life—and your writing.

But what do I have to say? you ask. No one believes in himself or herself overnight.

You keep practicing. You let Jimmy Santiago Baca be your guide. You take the side of Neruda and Lorca, Shakespeare, the great poetry, plays, novels, essays, that have come before you. Take the side of lit-er-a-ture, handed down through the ages. You are part of it. No credentials necessary. With your effort you step into the long river of awakened minds willing to reflect human suffering and glory. You are included with your fat pen and cheap spiral notebook, your grubby hands and dirty mouth, your seemingly dull experience and your seed of hope. Come one and all and manifest.

Enough said. What did you know in your heart one day in July 1990. Don't hesitate. Go, ten minutes.

Pull

Even if you're happily married now, tell us about that man or woman or that old lover you can't get off your mind. What's the pull? Go. Ten minutes.

Wild

Tell me how you were wild and green in the ways of the world. Don't think. Write ten minutes. Go.

The Addict

Often a slippery relationship exists between the real and unreal, between stories and facts. We want to read true examples but we want to be entertained. We don't like being bored. We are a hyped-up society, demanding bigger, faster, more. These real-life stories have to be filled with excitement, pathos, redemption. We exaggerate, embellish. So much pulls at us as writers—not the least the need to be accepted, successful, well-liked. But a writer also has a commitment to truth. We think that an insecure boy in his twenties is dull material. But if you write about him you have a texture, a love and hate to that young boy. The author's job is to convey this, even if that young boy you write about is yourself.

Certain memoirs have generated a lot of controversy, because, it was discovered, their authors had slanted some of their facts. For instance, an author who posed as a tough guy spent three hours in jail but wrote that he was there for three months. He also wrote that he had beaten up some other tough guys. An investigative group dug up legal records that disprove his version of these and other claims. This discrepancy undercuts the impact of the book as a whole. When you read the book carefully, you can tell that things don't hang together. The tough guy is an addict who comes from a soft upper-class background. Nothing in his history accounts for how he could suddenly have developed the physical prowess to beat up street toughs. There is too much bravado, too much wreckage that he writes about too eagerly.

Another memoirist pretended to be Native American. In his much more grievous misrepresentation, the whole premise and story were false. Native Americans were outraged at the disrespect toward their culture and misuse of it by a white author. But Native American news goes under the wire.

Because the Addict's book was very popular, when the lies came to light the whole country was in an uproar. Articles were in every paper. Journalists and columnists went for his jugular. Talk shows talked about him. One TV talk host, who had at first made him part of her book club, brought him on her show to denounce him and his falsehoods. "The truth will make you free," she said.

It was as though a channel had been broken open, an avenue to vent pent-up rage. Not one writer whom I read defended him. We all knew he had goofed. But why did everyone go this crazy? People became scared to write. They lost trust in memoir and their own ability to remember.

The Addict could be named, but we are talking about something bigger than one author at one time with one book. Also the poor boy should be left alone at this point to follow his lone trail into the sage and tumbleweeds.

Nowhere was it suggested that the reader take some responsibility for the situation, for being so upset. This author was an addict. It was naive of readers to believe everything he said. He lied and finagled and we read about it. Why didn't we also realize he was doing some lying to us?

But, you say, he went through recovery.

Recovery takes a lifetime. A few months in rehab is not enough. As readers we don't like to be duped. But we also need to use a discerning mind. The written word is not gospel. This was a story built with the help of imagination, memory meeting human needs and desires.

Many people were inspired by the book. The author had become a poster boy for recovery. When we heard he had lied, it burst our bubble. Hearing his lies made the difficulty of freeing ourselves from addiction more real. Even if an author who inspired us has lied, that is no excuse to hinder our own healing.

Recently I met a poet I'd admired for more than twenty years. In particular I loved a poem he'd written about his cousin Arthur, who spoke Spanish and had had a vision while looking out at the Hudson River. I'd read the poem aloud many times. I'd think about Arthur, wondering how he was now and where his life had taken him.

Soon after I met the poet, I asked: "How is your cousin Arthur?"

He looked at me oddly. "There's no Arthur. I made it up."

"You made it up?" I almost fell over.

Nowhere did it say that poetry had to be fact, but I had grown attached to Arthur and was certain—never even questioned—that he had to be a person. I had thought that, in poetry, the people, places, and situations were stationary and then you took a little leap into inspiration. But I was wrong. The poet was in his seventies. He'd been writing poems seriously for more than forty-five years. Of course, he had to go beyond the confines of who and what he knew.

Do I still love the Arthur poem? Yes, but it took a little time to readjust. We love what we love. Disillusionment is part of the loving. Getting closer, more real with what is. The poet did not hide his fabrications. He took it for granted that it was part of his art.

But memoir is different from a poem. It is created out of memory. It's okay to say it was a blue dress when it might have been purple or gray. We can eat rye and recall later with certainty that it was sourdough we had popped in the toaster. Memory has vagaries. We know that. But memory doesn't fabricate whole scenes that didn't exist. That's not called memory, but fantasy. What we make up also reveals things about ourselves, but usually we put those creations into novels, short stories, songs, and poetry. Even if you name the wrong town or the wrong shoe, those are incidentals. The problem with the Addict's work was that he had slanted the whole book. The things he wrote incorrectly were essential to understanding the story.

The Addict lost a great opportunity to get real with himself. The truth of what happened might have been even more cogent and compelling than what he wrote in order to make himself look cool and badass. What was really going on in those unaccounted three months when he said he was in jail? That's what we want to know. We have to trust that our experience as it is is valuable enough to write about. And, it can include fantasy. But you have to name it as fantasy. We like to feel that an author is in control of his material, not lost in it. The Addict moved over to delusion because he presented himself as a tough guy, rather than saying, "I wanted to be a tough guy." That would have made him more vulnerable and sympathetic.

You can develop the right compass to reach emotional truths inside your own life without having to fabricate your experience. Your life is good—or bad—enough. Your suffering is real.

Here is where the development of a tender heart helps. If you can have compassion for this man they are dragging over hot coals, you can have a tenderness also toward yourself. Mistakes are possible, you can whisper in your own ear. Go ahead anyway. You wanted to write. Go ahead, you encourage yourself.

Why was the Addict jumped on so much? He was on all the bestseller lists; he was successful. He had no credentials, no colleagues, no support system in place. He was an easy target.

Also, our country was in an unpopular war. It was a painful time. We were hearing of political deceptions; a favorite city in the South, New Orleans, was wiped out by a hurricane. We felt impotent. At least let a memoir, something close to our heart, be true. When we learned it wasn't, the bottom fell out. We were ravenous. The Addict became the scapegoat.

There is another reason his life story had such an explosive effect: he expressed a core truth about being driven, obsessed, hounded by our demons. In his angst, he turned to drink, but drink or not we all can relate to being possessed by those hounds gnawing at our throat. No rest, no peace. That nibbling dissatisfaction at the edge of consciousness. All of us have been harried, crazed, tormented. Mostly we live with it in quiet—or not so quiet—misery. But the author exposed an undeniable, essential nerve in us, which we should recognize along with his prevarications. Maybe he wasn't even aware of the torment he had captured; he might have backed into it by accident. But his expression of pain, his ranting, works. He expresses some human howling.

Polite

The things that make you a functional citizen in society—manners, discretion, cordiality—don't necessarily make you a good writer. Writing needs raw truth, wants your suffering and darkness on the table, revels in a cutting mind that takes no prisoners, wants to hear about an abortion, a broken heart, a failed job, a lost opportunity.

How much exposure, how much truth are you comfortable divulging in your memoir? Understand clear writing demands you to go beyond your usual threshold. There is no judgment. It's up to you.

What are you not willing to reveal? Go, ten minutes.

Repair

What have you tried to repair? Ten minutes. Go.

Awake

What tortures you and awakens you at night? Go for ten.

Nothing

Tell me in ten minutes why nothing worked, why you felt stuck where you were. Don't complain. Give me the specifics. You've been over this before? Go over it again. This time in writing. Get it down clearly so you never have to do it again. Boring, you say. Sometimes writing can be that way, but the details that seem ordinary to you are often strange and curious to someone else. Go. Ten minutes.

Facing It

There are times when monkey mind is screaming so loud you can't think. No understanding of it helps. Here then is a helpful device: give monkey mind space to let it rip. Give her a voice. Go. Ten minutes.

When I do this, I am surprised to find monkey mind is very redundant: *I hate you. You're stupid. You're dumb. You can't write. You're nobody. I hate you; you're stupid; you're dumb.*

She doesn't have much of a repertoire, but she can fill pages with a lot of energy. Imagine if we could harness her vigor. But for the time being, whenever she is in this state, it's best to give her some expression, see what she has to say. There are usually some truths thrown in with the ranting, but often delivered in an unsavory way.

Finally, if she won't quiet down, give her menial tasks: licking stamps, driving to the post office, buying dog food and toilet paper. Give her something to do. She'll explode otherwise.

Writers need the power and intensity of monkey mind. Her rant is an expression of human suffering that comes out powerfully when we pick up the pen. But we need skill to work with her. A little poison can cure, but a lot destroys. We can become engulfed by her, crushed by her driving force. People often point to the alcoholics, the depressives, the suicides that writers become, which may be the result of relentless, unbridled monkey mind. They get stuck with that constant driving voice inside.

But here you have a container: ten minutes. Go for it, monkey mind. Say everything you've been dying to say. Let's hear you. You have the floor. What destruction and wisdom can you mete out?

All this energy is yours. Don't run from it; don't become enveloped. Stand your ground. Only what you don't know, what you won't look at will destroy you. But also don't hand over the reins. Monkey mind is not you. It's a part of you, a mechanism in the mind. You run the show. You, who move the pen across the page.

Boring

Let's try a preventive for lying. Even though you think your life as it is is insipid, flat, bland, not good enough for the realm of memoir, try slowing down even more. Go beyond how tedious things already seem. Take something so boring you never want to be caught doing it, much less writing about it.

Let's take dusting. You dust your cabinet once a week. What do you dust it with? Where did you get those paper towels—or that old plaid square of material? Where do you think all this dust comes from? When did you get that bureau? What day, hour do you dust? How is dusting different in summer and winter? What if you skipped three weeks? What is something odd you realize about dusting now that you think of it? Did you ever tell anyone you did this every week?

Get the idea? Get closer to what seems mundane instead of going away from it. Grow more intimate. Vitality exists right here in your life. Contact it, wake up to it.

Make a list of ten witless activities that you do. During the week do a ten-minute write about seven of them. The other three? Let them continue in their humdrum way. You'll need some ammunition, some potential, left in your holster. A little place where the energy is building.

But here's a question: what keeps you from acknowledging the dusting, the daily cooking, the night job you have? What dream did you have in your heart? Maybe under everything, the damn cleaning is driving you nuts because you wanted something else. What was that? Let's discover it. The writing will take you there. Ten minutes: if you weren't dusting—and worrying about your children—what is it you would like to do?

Ordinary

I've said this in subtle ways, but yesterday after a book reading an old student sidled up, not looking at me, and said, "My childhood wasn't so bad. I mean, well, I was brought up in Illinois—"

"You mean, what if I had an uneventful, ordinary life, can I still write a memoir?" I cut in.

She nodded shyly.

"You know the answer. What did Mies van der Rohe say? *God hides in the details.* Slow down and give them to us. We need to read about regular childhoods; otherwise, we won't know what they are. We'll never know what direction to head."

A tremendous relief flushed across her face.

We need you—the ones who had a cough and your mother or grandfather was there to administer the syrup. Even if you had only one year when you were three when you tasted peace, let us know about that. The experience probably gave your fragile life a foundation. Share that ground with us.

Maybe you were a great mother or father. Tell us what that was like—what went into the effort—and where did it come from?

The important thing is to go below the clichés to touch the texture of your experience. Your mind is hungry to be alive. You give us that gift by laying down your true mind on the page. We read it and you open up fields of our own imagination.

Thank you for this. Thank you for whatever you have lived. It all passes. Let it have its time.

Something

Go. Find something ordinary and tell us about it.

Swim

Make sure that swimming is somewhere in your memoir. Why? I don't know. It seems a memoir needs a splash of water. For now give us ten minutes of it. Go. Tell us something about swimming.

Of course, swimming can lead to drowning. When did you feel you were drowning? Go. Another ten.

Poor

How poor were you? Go. Ten minutes.

Lie

We lie for a hundred reasons. We're no good, no one likes us, we should have been born in Paris. We don't like our skin color, our eyes, nose, teeth, chin. We are fat, plain ugly, our parents' politics suck and we're ashamed.

I used to encourage students to lie, to exaggerate in order to shake them out of their predictable ways of seeing things. Obviously, these techniques can be dangerous with memoir. Instead fall in love with your life. This does not mean you can be blind and insipid: Yippee! I was raped. How lovely to be mugged. The war wasn't so bad after all. Rather, be caring, interested, curious about these ups and downs, vicissitudes, trials of your existence. Name them with no judgment.

Mistake

Tell me about the worst thing that has happened to you. Go, ten minutes.

Tell me about the best moment you've experienced. Go, ten minutes.

Tell me what your biggest mistake has been. Go, write for as long as you want.

Weather

Of course, you should throw in weather as you write about your brother, how it was raining out the day you finally realized he was always going to be better in school than you, that no teacher would praise you the way they did him. Or it was snowing out the last time you saw your grandfather. He was lying small and broken in his bed and the flakes were big and slow out the window.

Weather is a rich and important quality in writing, because it's a real and affecting thing in human life. Lace it through your work.

Right now write for a full ten minutes about some big weather you experienced. A tornado, a hurricane, an ice storm where the hail was as big as golf balls.

You say you live in the tropics. All the weather is the same. You are right: one big phenomenon of heat. Write about it.

All you can remember is one bland gray week when you went to the shore and it was supposed to be sunny and you were supposed to be having a vacation. Gray is good. Within bland is discovery. Go inside it and find something.

Fantasy

Sometimes we just want to lie. I meet a woman I'll never see again at a swimming pool. "How many children do you have?" she asks, never imagining the number zero.

"Oh, four," I say. "Two still home, one married, and one in his junior year at Northwestern." I smile with pleasure.

What fantasies can you admit to? Make a list and then write about them. They can be included in your memoir. In fact, the fantasy will enrich the memoir, as long as it is obvious it's fantasy, because it reveals a different aspect of your mind.

In *The Woman Warrior* Maxine Hong Kingston wrote a long chapter about her fantasy of being a great female warrior. The fantasy came straight out of her Chinese background, and juxtaposed with her Chinese American childhood, set up a backdrop, intensifying the portrait of her Chinese mother. It is very effective and fresh.

But in passing I should confess to you that I don't really have four children. I have eight—all demanding my attention. There's Cooking, Writing, Yoga, Politics, Painting, Hiking, Teaching, Swimming, Going to the Movies. Recently I sent Going to the Movies to prep school. She was getting out of hand. I knew a good teacher there who would instruct her how not to eat so much popcorn. Last week she sent me a letter: all A's except in loving her mommy. There she received an F.

Vice

What was the secret vice you held close? Go. Ten minutes.

Hand and Wrist

Tell me about someone's hands. Maybe forget about the hand altogether. Can you tell me about his wrist? Was it hers that tipped the scale and made you fall in love? Wrist, what an odd and wonderful word, when you think about it. Ten minutes. Go.

Jump

Tell me about a time you knew glory. Go. Jump in. Write ten minutes.

Care

When did you pretend not to care? Go. Ten minutes.

Test IV

Three minutes on each of these topics. Stay with details.

____A memory of bread and butter

____A memory of drinking out of a bottle

____A hill you once knew

____A recollection of mist

____A moment in a library

Cezanne

Ten years ago I saw a big Cezanne show in Philadelphia. The lines to get in were long. The galleries were crowded. You viewed a painting behind six other people. You bent your head this way and that to see portions of the pictures between people's arms, torsos, and heads. I liked the paintings but I knew I was missing something. Printed matter said Cezanne influenced generations of artists, that all subsequent famous painters had looked to him. Cezanne painted mountains and streams, some portraits. Other artists before him did that. What was the big deal?

When I went home to New Mexico I asked my painter friend to explain. She tried. I didn't understand, but I held the question inside.

Then just recently I attended a show of Pissarro and Cezanne, side by side. The two painters had been friends, often going out to the country together and setting up easels next to each other.

I was jet-lagged and groggy when I entered the museum after again waiting in a long line where I spoke to a man from Las Vegas. He'd brought his eighty-year-old mother to Paris and she was too tired. He left her back in the hotel.

The minute I saw Pissarro next to his friend Cezanne the answer to my question from ten years ago sprang at me, looming large, barefaced in the room. Pissarro's paintings were well-done, but he followed an old idea of perspective. They receded the way we were taught in grammar school that a picture should move away to a distant point to give it depth. Next to Pissarro, Cezanne's came right at you. There was no distance. If it was a water scene, the water came to the edge of the canvas. You were in the water. You were included.

Two paintings of bouquets hung side by side. Pissarro showed the edge of the table and divided us from the bouquet. Cezanne stuck the flowers right in my face. I could almost smell them. Before I'd seen Cezanne only by himself and since so many painters after him followed his way, I could not tell the new thing he had done. But compared to his contemporary I could see how he'd stepped right through the old manner of seeing and broken open perspective. The experience was exhilarating.

The show centered on their friendship. How they both painted the same bridge together; then a bunch of apples in a still-life. What conviviality. But I wondered what it must have been like for the two of them standing side by side, glancing over at the other's easel.

"Has Cezanne lost his mind? He needs to go back to school and learn to draw." Pissarro was the older.

And Cezanne, whose dedication, suffering, and loneliness are famous, must have felt sure of himself in the way changing reality can free you but also make you insecure. No one else had done this. And no one was going to applaud. Pissarro's work standing next to him must have only intensified the difference.

I noticed Cezanne used looser, larger strokes, brought out the intensity of one color, did not soften the blow, was angular, took more chances. I'd waited ten years to see what I was seeing.

I took a breath. I knew this also applied to writing.

Can you do the same? Bring your experience forward. Don't bog down in long introductions or explanations. Crash through what holds you back.

Also know sometimes you have to wait a long time for understanding.

Let's try this: Tell me what stifles you. Throw in everything that might even be a possibility. Go. Ten minutes.

Now that you've cleared the way, what is it you want to say? Step forward. Speak it upfront with no explanations. Go. Another ten minutes.

What must you be patient about? Make a list to remind yourself.

Apples

Exactly how do you feel about apples?
    What is your impression of plums?
    When was the last time you peeled a tangerine?
    Can you eat five ripe peaches in a row?
    Why did summer mean so much—and the last two summers
fail you?
    You guessed it. Write about all this. You pick the amount of
time. Go.

Joan Mitchell

This is not the Joni Mitchell who is the famous singer/song-writer, who paints as a hobby, and once tried to visit Georgia O'Keeffe in Abiquiu, New Mexico. This Joan Mitchell started out as a poet, was brought up in Chicago, moved to France, and painted large abstract oil canvases, inspired by nature. Her paintings held their own alongside her peers and forebears such as Jasper Johns, Cy Twombly, and Willem de Kooning.

Most women of that time who were successful had a man connected to them—either a famous painter husband or a rich spouse backing them. It does not mean these women were not fully talented on their own—it was that the times were difficult for women artists.

Joan Mitchell did it on her own. Her dedication and determination were not deterred. She died in 1992.

The Whitney Museum of Art had a huge retrospective of her work in 2002. A friend told me that the viewers were six deep, gathered around her paintings. I wanted to go very much but was not able to travel to New York at that time. After New York the show was exhibited in Fort Worth, Texas.

Flying home from having Thanksgiving with my mother in Florida, I had to change planes at the Dallas/Fort Worth airport. Unplanned, without thinking, I was heading for the exit. I knew those paintings were a few miles away. I rented a car and drove the forty minutes to the new Modern in downtown Fort Worth. I prayed my luggage would be waiting for me whenever I got to Albuquerque. I parked in the empty lot—it was a Sunday. The air was filled with the smell of manure from the slaughterhouses nearby. I ran excitedly to the front door. I was the only one in the galleries. I swirled round and round, running from one painting to the other.

All at once a man appeared at the far end. "Natalie?" he said and my name echoed through the rooms.

I stopped.

"I'm your old student," he said. He came closer. "Remember? I studied with you two years ago. I'm from Kansas. I drove to my brother's for the holidays—he lives near here—and I'm heading home."

What a stunning coincidence. Standing side by side we stood and stared up at bright yellows, oranges, and blues splashed across canvases. Two waifs in the empty rooms.

After he left I went to the Museum bookstore and read how she died of cancer, that even near the end, she'd lie in her studio and her only motion for a day would be to drag herself up a ladder to add a spot of orange on a painting she felt was unfinished. "There!" she'd pronounce, satisfied.

As I read I saw that her life was tough, that she was an alcoholic, that things did not come easily for her.

I turned the pages of the big art book and came to a painting done in 1992 right before she died. Purple, blue, and orange played with one another on both sides of a diptych against vast white. The painting held me and I stopped turning the pages. So much play and freedom, such strong strokes and yet you felt the whole thing could evaporate like a cloud. My eye ran to the bottom corner of the page. There was a single word in French for the title: *"Merci."* My body reeled backward. Tears sprang to my eyes. I translated in a quiet voice, "Thank you." I said it again, "Thank you. Thank you." She had lived and she had died and she did not regret. Her memoir was one last word; one last painting.

Vast Affection

What will your last word be? You cannot answer this off the top of your head. Let the answer come from someplace other than your thoughts—let it rise like a dead fish from the bottom of the ocean, from the center of your belly.

What are you thankful for? Deep down full of vast affection? Ten minutes. Go.

No

Begin a ten-minute writing with *No Thank You*. Every time you get stuck, write *No Thank You* again and keep going.

Ahead

When did you know you were going to suffer but went ahead anyway? Go. Ten minutes.

Sickness

Don't forget about sickness. Write about a whopper of a flu, pneumonia, a cold, sore throat, eye infection, stomachache. We don't necessarily want to hear all the gory details but begin with them if you need to and see where it leads. Sickness is often an untouched subject, but it exists for all of us. We are all affected. Make your writing human, include allergies, muscle aches, a bad knee.

Try disease. This is scarier. Often it's linked with impermanence, fatality. Tell us about a disease you or someone you love has or had. Go ten minutes.

Driving

Let's talk about driving. How did you learn? What kind of driver are you? Be specific: tell me about a route you drive regularly, give the turns, the scenery, stoplights. When was driving fun? We are looking here for things we take for granted, that go unnoticed. We are trying to wake up to ourselves.

You can say, this is a waste of time, you need to write about the flood in your hometown that devastated everyone. Go ahead, sink into that. Write everything you can think of. Urgency is good. Get it down on paper. That's important.

But then take a breath. Memoir is not reportage. Memoir examines how one thing leads to another, how human life—in this case, yours—unfolds. Describing your drive to the grocery, the dentist, or work can magnify what has been destroyed in the flood. It's playing with the positive and negative, not as bad or good, but in this case what was and is no longer.

Window

What was outside your bedroom window? Go for ten.

Paris

Tonight in Paris I walked to dinner at Trumilou's, the restaurant I first went to twenty-two years ago. Each time I visit this city I find my way here. A small modest café on the Seine with inexpensive good food and a sparkling black and white linoleum floor. I did not expect to be so filled with emotion as I bent over my *salade verte,* still with the same mustard dressing. I came here with my friend Carol the September there was a bomb scare in Paris and they cut off all entries to the city. We somehow managed our way from Lisbon. We met John and Beverly from Minneapolis. They didn't yet have their two beautiful children. John was learning French. Beverly was yet to write her book of short poems she called stories.

But I also came to Trumilou's on other visits—with Cynthia after a retreat in Plum Village, with Barbara Zaring, the painter, Geneen and Matt, my Nebraska friend Barbara Schmitz. We were all younger. What did it feel like to be in our thirties, our forties? I've been to many favorite restaurants, but why this night does everything feel so dear? I can recall each water glass, peach melba, face, mouth, spoon, bill on the tray, hand groping for a wallet.

This is the hard trick: I feel sentimental, but if I write it that way, the images and events are a closed circuit. They flounder in my own pleasure but don't reach out. This is okay if it is what I want to do, but it will stay in my journal. Don't bother to type it up. It's something private.

Memoir is taking personal experience and turning it inside

out. We surrender our most precious understanding, so others can feel what we felt and be enlarged. This means when we write we give up ourselves. I make that restaurant—that time, place, precious age—public, not mine any longer. But this does not mean to write about it in a grand manner. "Oh, life was good. My friends were precious." It means getting as close as we can to every detail. The grain of the bread served up in a basket, the tall clear water bottle on the table, the ratty boar's head hanging across the room, the empty toilet paper container in the WC— as they call it—the water closet.

But even giving away all the details won't be enough. We have to be willing to take the next step, to somehow locate the muscle underneath. What throb, what beat, makes us love this place, carries us into the center of feeling?

Then we need drive and connection, a narration. It's not enough to tell you I was at Trumilou's with Carol, then another year with Cynthia, an earlier time with Barbara. What link brings it all together? You must discover that force—it's in you—and tear up the page with those smoldering moments, so the reader knows he has eaten in Trumilou's too, that Trumilou's has been also banging in his bones.

What is asked is not easy. You lose everything in the act of writing. Are you willing? It all goes down the drain anyway when we die. And I promise, we will die. Maybe the best thing is to be used up before we go.

What is it you love and are willing to give to the page?

It's why we write memoir, not to immortalize but to surrender ourselves. It is our one great act of generosity. To drop that old yellow coat of our needs and desires and give pleasure through stories.

Quiet

Tell me about silence. Go. Ten minutes.

All writers know about silence, even if they talk and chatter all the time. It's at their back. Silence drives them into the radiant light.

No Stop

What were some relentless dreams you had? Go. Ten minutes.

Birthday

Today is May second, the birthday of a friend. I'm in another country across the sea thinking of her—and this is what I realize: I've always known she was smart, her insights are breathtaking, and along with that she likes to shop, buy costume jewelry, chat about people's love lives. Sometimes it seems like she is two different people—one brilliant, heady and the other a bozo for odd fashion and gossip. But tonight I see I've been missing something. The other third: her deep and caring heart. It's the backdrop in front of which all her brilliance and drama get played out. You notice the first two thirds because they are flashy and active. The last third is quiet, ever present. You watch the puppet show—her gleaming green glass earrings, brooch planted on her left shoulder, her steamy intuition of why Claire keeps sleeping with the wrong man, how Zen walks the edge of obsessive cruelty, how retreat centers should serve eggs for breakfast instead of gruel, the weakness of Peter—he writes too little about the wrong women—her sharpness could seem like its own cruelty except it is backed by an abundant beneficence. Sure, she slaughters with her words, slices off heads, thoughts, but there is a splendor behind it. A net is woven and then evaporates. We settle in our seats and the real visit begins. I am worried about my mother. She listens carefully. She metes out some sane advice.

People are complicated. Don't expect to understand the whole of them. They are like the French language. They delude the American mouth. Those vowels, those breaths. You try to capture on the page a woman you love and she springs from your hand. The third you left out is the real third. You add it and it splits into an unknown fourth. Know whatever you say it will be incomplete. There will always be a dust mote, a bird hovering, a cloud drifting—something ungraspable.

Confident of the big secret you will never know, in the center of that ambiguity, draw one gesture, write one image of someone. Here's an example from my birthday friend: she's a Jersey girl. She will never forgive a transgression. It comes from that state's scrappy toughness—so close to the Big Apple—but a satellite. They have to fight for their territory. But then oddly she will make a sudden turn. She will welcome you back into her life after the worst transgression. It doesn't make sense. She will forgive the unforgivable.

Writing memoir is a kaleidoscope. Do not think you nailed something forever. That's reason to write one at thirty-two, at eighteen, at forty-five, even at twelve it is a good thing. One is not smarter, no age is better. Each knows something that will never be known again.

Lickety-split, write down the names of five people you know. Draw a gesture in words about each one of them.

Now choose one: What do you think you know about her—or him? Go, ten minutes.

Say

Often in the middle of a timed writing practice you feel mud-
dled, you are not really saying anything. Try this: don't even wait
to finish your sentence, right in the middle put a dash, then
write, "What I really want to say is," drop to a deeper level, and
keep going.

Or you can start right off with this as the topic: what I really
want to say is . . . Go. Ten minutes.

Ring

Write about your mother's jewelry. Go. Ten minutes.
Write about her shoes. Go. Another ten.

Mind

What's been on your mind? What have you carried and gnawed over? Go. Ten minutes.

Time

Tell me about a clock you've looked at a lot. Go. Ten minutes.

Close

Let's use the example of a person who is a voracious reader. She swallows books, one after the other. Good books, well-written, on wide expanses of subjects. She finishes one on the famine in Darfur and within a half hour is digging into the biography of Andrew Carnegie and the story of the American railroad. No sooner has she completed a thick one on John Lewis and civil rights does she dive into a French murder mystery. And she remembers what she's read. She's smart and knowledgeable.

If this person decides to write a memoir it is her chance to ask the question, what have I learned from all these books? And closer to the skin: why do I read so much? There is no justification required, only examination. How have all these black words on white pages formed my mind? Of course, we also want to hear about her favorites, how she discovered them, where was she when she read them. We do want to hear how the weight of the volume in her hand led her to this solitary engagement, but we want something else, too. We don't want a generalization about bibliophiles. "They read a lot of books. They wear glasses. They never go outside. They have a pallid complexion." What is this person really like? we want to know.

If one person gives us a true picture of her life of books, it will bring us closer to the intoxicating taste of devouring all those words, better than any dictionary definition. This is her chance to make her life comprehensible, to delight us with her experience, the utter concentration behind the covers of a book.

Do you see?—this is memoir. It goes further—right into

the mind. The baseball games you watch—or the women you are obsessed with—aren't quite enough. They are in the right direction. But then we want you. Who are you that loves movies, buys popcorn—or takes up waterskiing at sixty. It's like the glorious green leaves of summer and the golden ones in autumn but the trunk stands all through winter. What is the root that makes these leaves? Don't worry, there is no right or wrong, good or bad answer. Just how close can you get?

No Whining

We start to read *Moby Dick* or *Heart of Darkness, Speak! Memory, Second Sex, Native Son, Don Quixote* and ten pages into it, we decide it's too hard, it's boring, we don't like it. I'm sorry to say it does not matter what you think. Your opinion here isn't important. We would be called immature if after ten minutes of meeting someone, we said to him, I don't like you. And yet this is often exactly what we do when we encounter a few pages of a new book. Our job is to stay with the author's words and see what we can learn. Push through. It takes a while to settle into a book's territory.

Carry a book bag with you. Read while you are standing in line at the post office. Snatch a few pages on the bus. You can be transported to India, rather than being irked in the waiting room because your doctor is a half hour late for your exam. When you finally walk into his office, E. M. Forster is filling your lungs. You are in an exotic country as the doctor looks down your throat and into your eyes.

Reading has so many advantages. Not the least, it is relaxing. You have an experience of spaciousness. Other places and people unfold inside you. Leaning over pages, still and quiet, you are exercising that big muscle in your head. If you keep toning it, it won't become flabby, while all your other appendages hang south. And when you read, you might forget to eat—you are busy rowing up the Nile, crocodiles snapping at your oars. Has anyone before mentioned reading's dietetic benefits?

March off to that library—or bookstore—right now: thousands of adventures and friends await you.

For a time you might want to read memoirs exclusively. Where did the author begin? How did he end? What did you miss and want to know more about? What details did she bring out? What is the structure of the book? How can this memoir inform yours?

Sometimes writers find that once they actually begin writing their book, they can read any genre but the one they are working in. But don't think a novelist hasn't read many novels, a poet, many poems, and a memoirist, many memoirs.

One more thing: If you read, you model a beautiful thing. Your children will notice, whether they run to read a book right then or not. Talk to them about the book you are reading. Read a bit aloud. Even if they don't understand it all, you are speaking to them.

Reading Life

Tell about periods when you haven't read. What were you doing? Ten minutes.

Where and when do you read best? Ten minutes.

If you want people to read your work, shouldn't you, also, be reading theirs? And I don't mean an even exchange: my friend read my book; I'll read his. Read McCullers's and your cousin's novels; read the poems of a man who just returned from China; read ten contemporary memoirs. It's like pausing in tall grass; let books grow up between your toes.

Long

What have you waited a long time for? Go. Ten minutes.

No More

What do you no longer have? Go for ten minutes.

Suicide

On January eleventh someone I loved died. He was in his mid-fifties. I wept hard when I heard. There were still things I had to say to him, an apology was one of them—for how I'd treated him long ago. I thought there was time, that the right opportunity would eventually come along. I didn't know he was sick.

Three days after the announcement of his death I received a phone call: "It was suicide." That word stopped neuron transmissions in my brain. I had such clear grief—and then this? I couldn't put the pieces together. If you gave me the names of a hundred people, he would have been the last one I'd think would go this way. I didn't know the circumstances and his wife was keeping silent. I didn't blame her. I tried to piece scenarios together. He loved his family—no problem there. He built a great business and loved it. He must have been terminal. I didn't know anything for sure.

I'd find myself talking to him while I walked down the street: Why didn't you call? I could have helped.

I'd eat a particularly good orange: you didn't want another orange? Bob, you didn't want to see March again?

Months passed and I stood outside a Paris train station. My friend had gone in to get tickets. I was guarding our luggage. Bob had taken a trip to Europe fifteen years earlier with three friends. Was it when they were in Paris? Prague? Amsterdam? At the train station watching their luggage, with his eyes wide open, his red valise was swiped. He could not say how it happened. I remembered this and was extra vigilant over three suitcases, two crammed backpacks, a laundry bag, and my purse.

Just near the sidewalk, a cab pulled up to the curb and right away three women with heads covered and five small children crowded around it. The one in a beige coat tried to shove a folded baby carriage into the trunk. The driver came out and he and the woman argued while the rest of the group piled into the two backseats. Clearly the carriage wouldn't fit. The buggy was pushed in and out from every angle. Finally it fell into place—the trunk was slammed shut, the woman and the driver hopped into the front, and the taxi edged into traffic.

So far my things were safe. Suddenly he was right there. I don't know how to say this: Bob was in a big place now, outside human dimension. How odd—in a dirty, frantic railroad station in another country where I understood none of the language except to order cheese, water, omelette, and ask where the toilet was, I experienced him again. No disagreement was between us anymore, no misunderstanding. No forgiveness necessary.

Another car pulled up—this time a convertible with the top down. A fancy French woman in heels, her long blonde hair tied back, came out from the driver's seat and tried to lug a black duffle from the trunk. Her daughter (they looked alike) lunged from the passenger side and dragged the canvas bag to the curb where a young girl, who wore a long braid down her back and looked like neither of them, stood. The driver bent and kissed the child many times on both cheeks and the child stood still and suffered the kisses.

Taking your life was something I knew nothing about. But on this Friday in a foreign city I was free of judging how anyone might go out. We all go one way or another and I felt at peace with that and with the person I once knew as a human being.

Do you know someone who committed suicide? Write about it. Go for ten.

Have you ever felt like committing suicide? Go, ten minutes. Write about it.

So little is understood about suicide. If we write about it, the center of our writing is about something unknown, unexplainable. Begin from this shaky place and see where it leads.

Also notice: I wasn't sure in which city my friend lost his suitcase. I could have made a guess. If it's an educated guess, sometimes that's okay. It fits the picture properly. Or you can say, "I'm not sure, I think it was . . ." or you can use the word *imagine* or its equivalent. "I imagine he left it in Prague." But this time I wanted to name the different cities he was in. It seemed more important than only the one where he lost something.

It's your call, when you write. Trust the urge inside to lead you to the right choice.

Times

Tell me about times you've been alone. Go. Ten.

Fish

Tell me about a time you ate salmon. Or caught one. Or bought
a pound. Go ten minutes.

Give Up

What can you give up knowing? Go for ten.

Death

We have polite words for death in order to comfort ourselves—
*he passed on, she joined her maker, the angels came for him, she is no
longer with us.* In this human dimension, we try to find language for what we are not sure of.

Much speculation occurs about what happens when we die, but no one can guarantee the afterlife experience, simply because no one has died and lived to talk about it. Yes, we have death experiences but no one's dead and gone—solid buried six feet under—and come back. We have religions that tell stories from thousands of years ago and we can decide to believe them—or not.

But here we are with pen in hand, trying to give language to experience we don't know. Writing, even when you write about death, is about the living. We are using human language to convey human experience. A blade of grass, a cup of milk experiences death a whole different way—though probably it's not much of a concern to them to express it. Those lucky dogs. But here we are, memoir in mind, trying to scratch out a story and in this case say something about someone dying.

Begin by giving some poignant details of the life of the person who died. Even better, the poignant interactions—good or bad—between you and that person. What was it like? Open up the dimensions of these people. Usually we are alone with our grief. Writing can give you the wicked idea that you can have company, at least for a little while. If you tell about his life, we can better feel his death. Go. Ten minutes.

Here's something from my notebook:

We hunted squirrels together in Kentucky. When Tom cooked them he said it tasted like chicken, but I knew it wasn't chicken. It was a state I'd never been in before and Tom, tall, thin with a brown moustache, loved hunting. A year before he taught me to make clay pots in Detroit in his backyard. He was patient and excited for me to learn. He loved to heat up the coals on the woodstove and drive around the broken streets in his red pickup. We seemed to talk about everything together but I knew there was a whole country of experience he never mentioned. I thought it was about Kentucky and the dried cornfields.

When Rob called me on a gray Saturday in New Mexico to tell me Tom OD'ed on heroin I knew the country was on no one's map. My mouth went dry and I couldn't speak. I fingered the only green pot I kept from those days. I wanted to throw it across the room and smash it. I also wanted to keep it whole.

Don't forget to include death in your memoir. It makes life more brilliant. Be straight about it and yourself. If you are afraid, say it.

Sex—or Money

While we are speaking about death, we should not forget its opposite—sex, the life force. But it's a squirmy subject. We either exaggerate or hide. But you don't need to expose everything right off. Begin writing about it in your secret notebook.

How do you feel about sex right now? Ten years ago?

Who was your best sexual partner? Why?

What is the hesitation, the pain, the panic you feel as you write?

Keep your hand moving for the full ten minutes. Yes, eating ice cream, dancing, a good conversation, painting, a deep eight hours of sleep can be as good as sex—but what are you avoiding?

You have no plans to touch sex in this memoir, you say. It's about travels to Spain, seeing your grandchild for the first time. Think about it. What doesn't have sex at its core? What doesn't bloom from love and the life force? Your very need to remember comes because you are alive. It's not that you must deliver a hot scene while writing about purchasing your first radio or CD player, but you need to know that something is pulsating. The trees, the birds are not afraid of it. The valleys sing of it. If you blank out on it, something will be missing in what you write. I guarantee it.

Another subject people hide as much as sex and keep secret is money. Often people will tell their most awful or terrific, their first or last sexual experience before they tell you how much money they have in the bank. It's as if telling someone how much you make or how much you will inherit is exposing your final defense. Give up that secret and you've thrown away all security. You might as well call in the armies, the tanks. You are about to be crushed.

You do not have to write on a small piece of paper the sum total of what you're worth and then quickly swallow it. Instead, explore what money is to you.

How did your family handle it?

Do you overspend or are you thrifty?

What's the cheapest you've ever been? The most generous? What can you never imagine buying? Go. Ten minutes.

How about backing into sex in the middle of this monetary exploration—where were you when you were extravagant, was it linked to sex? Go for ten minutes. Let it all hang out.

Don't worry, your exact financial budget probably doesn't make for great writing—and neither does explicit sex. It's the story, the innuendoes around money and sex that interest us. But you have to begin somewhere. Begin with your allowance in fifth grade and see where it takes you. Go, ten minutes, keep the pen moving.

Fat

Here is something from *Fat Girl* by Judith Moore:

> I walked into the hall and saw into Uncle Carl's bedroom, and he and Jon were stretched across the chartreuse bedspread and they were naked except for boxer shorts, and they were kissing and didn't see me or hear me. By the bed on the chartreuse scatter rug, I saw four empty Grapette bottles and I knew, then, there wouldn't be Grapette for me.
>
> I didn't know what to think about the kissing, I really didn't. I didn't mind. And, in fact, I lied just now. They actually were naked and I put them into boxer shorts so that you wouldn't be shocked or disgusted. But I truly didn't mind. I'd seen butts before. I'd seen kissing.

Take note of how she switches direction in the second mid-paragraph and tells you she lied in the earlier paragraph. We get the chance to watch her mind in action, her process of walking in on a sexual experience.

You can make a statement and then show your refinement of it. This can add texture and nuance, also a sense of pause, a feeling of space. We are watching the dropping of thoughts onto paper. Mostly we simply become absorbed as we read. Here there is a reminder—oh, yes, a mind is speaking to us. It helps to create intimacy.

Of course, you must be careful. Exposing too much of your thinking can get tedious:

She was pretty. Well, kind of cute with red freckles. Maybe she wasn't cute. Maybe I just liked freckles. I don't know. I touched her. Then I decided to pull away. I thought that I liked her. Maybe I didn't. She reminded me of Lana Turner from old movies. I don't know why I said that. I don't watch old movies. Lana Turner didn't have freckles. Or she covered them up with a lot of makeup. She was pretty—and half ugly and half I felt mixed up.

Right here I tried to make up some lines to show how tiresome it can get to disclose too much of your thinking, but what seems to be displayed instead is a neurotic way of thinking. We all know that kind of mind, that can't decide, can't ground itself. This is a whole different thing from Moore's two paragraphs. Those are in control. But in this paragraph we have something different—swimming and blathering in our noodly mind. This mind always is waiting backstage for a chance to come forward and have its day.

Let's give it space right now so it doesn't leak into our streamline story. Can you imagine an Olympic ice skater in the middle of her performance go on about a hot fudge sundae she wished she was eating. But come to think of it, it might be so original—and true—that she wins the gold.

Ten minutes, grab a topic, anything—walls, trees, bacon, a car engine, knees, the gross national product, homelessness, pregnancy, French wine. It doesn't matter if you know anything about it. Lots of people talk about what they don't know. We are all crazy and can spin out on anything given a chance. Here's your chance. Show the old craziness full blast. Ten minutes. Keep the pen moving. Go on about jockstraps. All your deranged thoughts. Backtrack, repeat, discard, or discredit the thought before.

Here's another line from *Fat Girl* near the end of the book:

You who are reading here may have an idea about why I lolled around June's apartment . . .

Moore turns around and addresses the reader directly. As you read along in her book it's rather startling to be addressed suddenly and directly. Here you are getting the inside skinny on someone's fat life, but all at once she tells you she knows you are there—and, in fact, thanks you at the end for keeping her company while she tells her story. It's a wonderful sensation as you read.

All of the above are ways to jazz up or add complexity to a straight linear story. There are many possibilities. Put in a curlicue of thought or a step forward and a step back, a turning to address someone directly.

You are writing along about your father. In the next paragraph switch and speak directly to him, say the things you never dared say before.

As a matter of fact, do that now. Ten minutes, go. Letter to your father.

Remember? There are no prescriptions in writing, no one way that will get you there forever. A little jig, a waltz, the cha-cha, the lindy, a polka—it's good to know a lot of moves, so when it's your time, which is right now, you can dance your ass off.

Obese

Ten minutes on being fat, chubby, flabby, stout, bulky, paunchy, pot-bellied, fleshy, blubbery, plump, round, or corpulent. Go.

Smoke

Take a line you've written about someone; for example, *she bit her lip when you talked to her.* Instead of going on to the next thing, linger with the lip for a while. Give a fuller picture.

It was the right upper lip. At first I thought she'd gotten food stuck between her teeth and was trying to jerk the bit of hamburger with her tongue. But it happened all the time. I'd see a sucked-in small piece of her mouth. We didn't know each other well at the beginning. I thought maybe it was a nervous habit. She had a beautiful mouth and big white teeth. Why wouldn't she show her mouth to the best advantage? Even after a few months, after we made love, when she was relaxed and happy, even right after laughter, the upper right lip was pulled in. I began to see it had nothing to do with me. It was an internal uneasiness. Half of her wanted to open up and the other half was held in. After awhile I could imagine her as an old woman with no teeth, the whole mouth collapsed into one wrinkled fat black hole.

Now you try. Write a sentence about someone you know. As a matter of fact, write three about three different people. Jujitsu, one after the other.

Then pick one. Don't contemplate which is the best. There is no best; there is only your willingness to get closer, more familiar, to look again and see what you see. Naturally, if you write about someone's eyes, you are not going to have those eyes in front of you—you might have known those eyes fifteen years ago. So what I'm asking you to do is get more intimate with your own mind—the instrument where the memory is carried. Sitting and writing this—in a café, in your backyard, on a bus, at your desk—the evocation of these exact details then touches feeling. The feeling may be horror, love, repugnance, desire. But there you have it—whatever the emotion, stay in there. See how far you can stretch that one detail. Keep your hand moving. Bring that picture—and feeling—to fruition.

Let's look at something Frank Conroy in *Stop-Time* wrote about his stepfather:

> He finished his coffee and cigarette slowly, savoring the mixed flavors and the moment of rest. Since he'd stopped using the holder his smoking style had changed. He'd take a quick drag, blow out about a third of the smoke immediately, inhale the rest, and let it come out as he talked. I often made it a point to sit in such a way that a strong light source behind him showed up the smoke. It was amazing how long it came out, a fine, almost invisible blue stream, phrase after phrase, changing direction smoothly as he clipped off the words. For some reason I admired this phenomenon tremendously. I could sit watching for hours.

It's satisfying, isn't it, to read this? We all recognize that smoke and the way it moved. Conroy took the time to nail it. We are all a little more awake because of what he did.

Chang-Rae Lee

You cannot be told enough that when you write, *slow down*. Capture the world that happens in each instant. Not every instant, but at least some. Don't rush over things. Here is Chang-Rae Lee remembering a moment of his mother's cooking after she died.

For *kalbi,* she would take up a butchered short rib in her narrow hand, the flinty bone shaped like a section of an airplane wing and deeply embedded in gristle and flesh, and with the point of her knife cut so that the bone fell away, though not completely, leaving it connected to the meat by the barest opaque layer of tendon. Then she methodically butterflied the flesh, cutting and unfolding, repeating the action until the meat lay out on her board, glistening and ready for seasoning. She scored it diagonally, then sifted sugar into the crevices with her pinched fingers, gently rubbing in the crystals. The sugar would tenderize as well as sweeten the meat. She did this with each rib, and then set them all aside in a large shallow bowl. She minced a half-dozen cloves of garlic, a stub of gingerroot, sliced up a few scallions, and spread it all over the meat. She wiped her hands and took out a bottle of sesame oil, and, after pausing for a moment, streamed the dark oil in two swift circles around the bowl. After adding a few splashes of soy sauce, she thrust her hands in and kneaded the flesh, careful not to dislodge the bones. I asked her why it mattered that they remain connected. "The meat needs the bone nearby," she said, "to borrow its richness." She wiped her hands clean of the marinade, except for her little finger, which she would flick with her tongue from time to time, because she knew that the flavor of a good dish developed not at once but in stages.

from *Coming Home Again*

Those ribs are immortalized—I want to go make them myself—and it's as enlivening to read about them as it would be to read of a motorcycle race.

If you've lived ten years, you have enough writing material for your whole life. If you're thirty years old, stop everything. You already have too much to capture. If you're sixty and your memories are fading, seven images—your mother's face, a cake from Ebinger's bakery, the feel of a football, a street you remember, the smell of gunshot, the first movie you loved, one time of heartbreaking sex—should fill a book. Just slow down.

Enamored

Tell me about a time you were instantly enamored. Go. Ten minutes.

At the Edge

Anyone alive has had great suffering, if we are willing to admit it. Can you also notice the great tenderness at its edge? Tell me about it. Go. Ten minutes.

Fight

Your memoir might be about your childhood as a lush. It began at seven taking sips from your aunt's beer. By ten it escalated to stealing bottles of wine and finishing them off all by yourself in the cellar when your parents worked nights. The story builds into your twenties. You look into your memories for a key to what all this was about. Intermittent for a decade from fifteen on there were scenes with your father. He is begging you to stop. So you show these scenes—one becomes chapter seven, another chapter twelve, eighteen, and twenty-three.

Here's the key: you can't give the same scene in the same way. If you need to hammer home the repetition of fights with your father—the memoir might even turn into you and your father as the central theme, the crux of the suffering—you still can't show those battles in the same way each time. Your readers will get bored. Pretty soon they'll even put down the pages and stop reading altogether. You, of course, don't want that.

Each fight has to be different, should enrich, add nuance, deepen our understanding. Even if the gist is the same, we don't want each one in the kitchen, your mother crying and the supper cold on the dinner table. Put us in different places, give us different angles. You should be increasing the reader's vision. Each confrontation should add information.

But they were the same, you say, and they drove you crazy.

You have to go deeper. Repeating the same thing will drive the reader crazy and they'll leave you. Let your mother do something else, rather than cry each time. Your mother probably had a range of emotions. As a kid we see things black and white. Explore your mother in chapter twelve even if the central action is still you and your father. In chapter eighteen there is an opportunity to describe the tiles around the kitchen sink, the geraniums and African violets on the window ledge, the linoleum (don't you love that word) and Formica, the blender, the refrigerator hum, the water glasses from a trip through Iowa, the oilcloth table, the salt and pepper shakers, the lousy broom in the corner, the dustpan, the awful yellow curtains.

But I didn't care about those things, you say, or notice them.

You didn't notice or care about anything then. You were drunk and acting out. Go back and find them. Not literally, of course, but in your mind. Stretch yourself. This writing is about discovering what you already know but don't know you know. If you give us only the mind of an adolescent drunk, it could get pretty bland.

How about in the next battle scene with your father, chapter twenty-three, you write about your missing brother. He disappears when these confrontations happen. He's up in his room studying. He is the A student. You hate his guts but you also want to be close. Suddenly it's complicated inside you. Things were easier as a blur, an alcoholic haze. Tell us about that.

Sure, we can even add a chapter twenty-nine—what you were hoping for all along—some true meeting with this man called father, some reaching through.

So you see, you have to keep adding additional texture. Give us the fullness of your life, even if you weren't aware of that fullness at the time. Discover its great capacity and its complete dimensions.

Don't forget how things smelled and tasted and felt. Use those senses.

The Fourth

Tell me a memory from the Fourth of July. Where were you?
When? What was the light like? Why this particular Fourth? Go.
Ten minutes.

Four Words

Take a breath. Yes, you will need to be determined—writing takes commitment. It also takes space—space to write and space to receive. I could tell you in four words what to do and it will hold you for your writing life. Do you want to know those four? *Shut Up and Write.* Maybe they should be your baseline, especially when you are lollygagging too much. But how can anything with that wonderful word, *lollygag,* be bad for you?

So you have your baseline, but the mind is vast. It tugs at you. Sometimes you follow and write down the wrong alley and get lost. You did not waste your time. You are learning the territory. Another tug and a larger picture is revealed. When a woman is pregnant, she knows she will have a baby. She cannot change her mind and decide to have a carrot. The course is set. Yet she can't have that baby in an hour or a week. The full gestation must take place. So it is with a book you write. The aim is clear. How you get there is another story. So *Shut Up and Write* and eat, make love, do your laundry, dance to a reggae band, have a nervous breakdown if you must, but continue. This writing is a path. It's about your life that never followed anything you planned. Look at where you are now. Whoever thought you'd be there? Forget your little will. It won't get you far. You'll manage to diet for a week and eat chocolate for a month.

Don't be hard on yourself. That makes your writing tight. Allow the luxury of time, dreaming out the window, a little noodle walk through a dime store, then like a female lion after her prey, go directly into the animal art of pen across paper.

Four Words

This chapter is for my friend who calls me wondering when I'll work on this book. I write a chapter and then go to the nursery to pick up zinnias for the garden. I write another chapter and go home and make soup. I know more but I don't push it because there are things I don't know that I want to come to me. I'm calling up understanding beyond myself. If I get too determined, too linear, I'll miss the tugs of intuition at the periphery of my perceptions, the things I don't want to say, the things I have never said, these things that enrich the writing.

Perfect

Was there a time you tried to be perfect? Go. Ten minutes.

Lucky

Let's try this one: how lucky have you been? Go. Ten minutes.

Spit

But sometimes you have to forget about space, time, and day-dreaming and you have to ignite on the page. A gun's at your head. You've got to get it done. You have one foot in the grave, or one hour at five a.m. before the kids wake and you have to get them to school and get yourself to work as an accountant, a mailman, a garbage collector, an executive at a dot-com. Who would ever believe that in the wee hours of the morning you were divulging your own secrets, claiming your own time, loving your spoiled and erratic life?

Sometimes you have to kick ass, home in, write like a mad-woman. You have no alternative. No choice. This can be a very alive situation. Your life like a snake has been placed inside a bamboo pole. No wiggle room. You have to spit straight ahead. Write! Don't think. Read the last sentence from the day before and Go!

Dresser

What was on top of your daddy's dresser? In the drawers? Or your uncle's, your grandfather's, your stepfather's, your mother's boyfriend's? Go for ten.

Test V

Three minutes on each of these:

____The best song of my life

____What I can't live without

____What I can't forget

____What I can't forgive

____At night I think of . . .

These are big topics to squeeze into three minutes, but it's good sometimes to snap to attention and get concise. One after the other, slice them open. Stay detailed.

Blind

What were the advertisements for cigarettes in the fifties? Exactly what is the training for a fireman? Who were the pop singers in the eighties? Precisely why did Bush invade Iraq? Who died in the Gulf War? Who shot King? Did we have a poet laureate in 1966? What ignited gay rights? What is the history of saving redwoods in the West? Do some research.

But once you have some facts don't act like a Miss Know-It-All. Explore the places where you kept yourself ignorant. Why did you protect yourself from the world? How come you were the president of a Southern sorority decorating ballrooms when the Vietnam War was raging and young men your age were being blown apart?

Juxtaposing the painful truth of genocide with the pop you were drinking at an all-day barbecue intensifies both. It's okay to let the world be big and painful. It's all happening at once. In the middle of it, you are searching for your salvation—don't you think there's some of that in your urge to write? Grace can't be found outside the truth of suffering. Go all the way in there when you write: the details of your thirtieth year and the details of El Salvador—or Nicaragua. Name your blindness and give it light. Go. Ten minutes.

Not Here

What was missing? Go. Ten minutes.

Politics

You can't get away from politics. The water you drink, the car you drive, the air you breathe are all connected to human inter-action, organization, association. There is the politics of the workplace, the government, the school, the church, mosque, synagogue. We don't like to think of our religious institutions as political—or our educational programs—but wherever human beings are interacting there is—for better or worse—a pull and tug. It's better to be aware of it. Blinding yourself gets you in trouble. Hemingway said the worst evil comes from innocence. All kinds of dark roots can be planted when you are not looking.

So what does this have to do with writing? An alertness to human beings' struggle for power, dominance, survival, justice, their inclination toward cooperation, longing for peace, gives a rubbing of elements, a narration to your work. A beautiful blade of grass all by itself is poetry. Enter a caterpillar—and there occurs drama, movement, interaction.

Beyond the periphery of our personal lives is the endless suf-fering and oppression of the human world. The countries in Africa, South America, the Middle East. The poverty in our cities, the intolerance across racial lines. This is about heart. Can we bear it? Can we go beyond logic and understanding into the incomprehensible? We write about the red wagon, the author we love, the slow spring we remember in Ohio, while at the same time atrocities, torture, genocide are happening. It's not wrong that our life has been graced, but it's important to acknowledge that while a rose blooms a bomb is being dropped. A writer must have a wide perspective, a stretched heart.

So should we write about the tanks invading a country as we tell about bringing our first quiche to the table? I don't know. Maybe no, maybe yes. It can create a tension, a wider scope, or it can be all wrong, not the right timing. But know that, at every moment, an atrocity is occurring. The important thing is to not turn your back on the immensity of the world's pain. Let it enter your life—don't open only to your own troubles, but leave room for unimaginable cruelty and devastation and know that, in some quiet corner of the universe, your individual hardship and theirs is linked. Knowing that maybe we all can find a way to include Lebanon, Israel, South Africa, Zimbabwe, the Philippines, Colombia, Afghanistan, Mexico—the list can go on—into our writing that is genuine and whole, making us genuine and whole, rather than artificial or duty-bound.

Several months ago I met my friend John Dear, a Jesuit monk and nonviolent peace activist, for lunch.

"John," I said, "I have been so happy these last weeks, for no reason. Gloriously happy—but then I think how can I feel this way with the suffering in Iraq."

He bent close, "Natalie, to be happy is revolutionary. You keep being happy. Oppressors do not want your happiness. They are geared to increase oppression."

Can we write with a touch of equanimity—not an ounce or hair removed, not coldly turned away, not surprised or taken aback? We have paid attention; we are not naïve. We know what one human being can do to another. And we, the writer, like a mother, gathering all her children onto the page, can write to include it all—the errant, the diseased, the quick-witted, the mean, the defiant, the outright cruel, the sweet and good.

We don't have to pretend any more that certain things don't exist.

My friend Eddie and I have a reading group about Africa that meets once every three months at the Travel Bug Bookstore in

Santa Fe. In March we assigned *We Wish to Inform You That Tomorrow We Will Be Killed With Our Families: Stories from Rwanda* by Philip Gourevitch. The author spent three years visiting Rwanda, trying to understand the terrible genocide that happened there, where seemingly overnight neighbor turned on neighbor and the Hutus slaughtered the Tutsis. Gourevitch lays out the entire development and history, precise, clear, intelligent, but even so there are parts in the book that are unbearable to read. You keep thinking, what is it to be a human being, are we capable of this, too? But oddly, when you finish, you feel almost exhilarated. Something so terrible and confusing, something you held as a dull blank blotch in your mind suddenly becomes absorbed, not shunned, not vague and incomprehensible.

Unfortunately, most of the twelve readers in the group couldn't bear to persevere. They couldn't get through the book; thus, they were downtrodden, stuck in pain when we gathered in our circle to discuss it. They missed the point. The ability to see, to move through, makes us more alive, awake on this earth.

I felt such appreciation for the author and his huge effort to bring clarity out of such pain and chaos that one morning out of the blue I called the *Paris Review* to speak to him. To my surprise, I got right through. I hadn't planned what to say and I gushed foolishly. He listened quietly and said, "Thank you," at the end. I'm certain I blushed, though no one saw me, and I hung up.

We have to be willing to see. The thing about peace is it is not unhinged from suffering. Right in the middle of the terror of the world we can pick up the pen and speak.

Not You

Here is a practice: spend ten minutes not thinking of yourself but only of the world, holding it, not taking sides.

On second thought maybe we'd better begin with three minutes and work up to ten. Not because the world doesn't deserve ten from us, but because our minds are so centered around the self that ten off the self all at once may damage circuits, make our straight hair curl, blow steam out of our ears. We hold a lot together all in the form of "I"; we unconsciously feel that the centrifugal center of gravity and the universe is us. We have to ease into the unselfish atmosphere, slowly come upon the definitive truth if it is to take hold: suffering is not personal.

So let's take it gradually like a serum: to begin with for three minutes, don't think about yourself. Go. See if you can do it. Normally in meditation, you are encouraged to think of nothing, to empty your mind. Here you are asked instead to change the scenery, freshen your thoughts with things that are not you.

Now for ten minutes, write about anything and everything that does not concern you. It's like airing out the brain.

What does this have to do with memoir? Memory is a large thing. We've been holding it back by our myopic self-referencing. Let's loosen its reins. See what it is capable of. We might leap into a whole new way to structure our own story.

Half 'n Half

I hope it is becoming obvious how topics for writing come up. They come out of your life and out of your surroundings, from a line in a book, a line in your head. They need to be concrete. The tangible world calls to you, makes you want to pick up a pen.

Public school had it all wrong with their topics:

justice
morality
liberty
freedom
education

These words are too big, too abstract. There is no juice.

Look at the difference. I glance around the café I am writing in:

half and half
sugar
cherry jelly
peppermint tea
Pepsi
lunch special
vodka
motorcycle
welcome

Do you feel how the specific pulls you in? The word "morality" makes the mind vague. Now give me "stealing" and I will probably end up writing about morality. Give me "morality" as the topic and I'll say it's a good thing and my mind will blank out. As a matter of fact, beware of the man who can pontificate about morality. He will probably steal you blind.

Let's look at the topic: half and half. It can have many meanings. Using this topic, your writing has many possibilities, can go off in many directions. There is the small container of half and half in front of you for coffee, the half in love and half not, half you want to be a writer, half you are pulled to be a dermatologist.

Here are examples of other topics that have different dimensions—meaning the concrete *and* the abstract, the tangible and intangible. Really, they are half 'n half.

Scars you've had—physical ones/ones inside
What you carry—in a purse, a backpack/what you carry inside
Drive—what you drive/what drives you
What you pay—coins, bills, dollars/pay with your guts, heart

Write about these for ten minutes.

Now write about what you don't carry, what you don't drive, what is not driven, what you don't pay, what is not scarred for ten minutes.

Place

Where were you born? Where do you live now? How did you get there? Of course, you can relate the logic: you moved to Iowa for a job. But tell me also on a deeper level: when did moving and restlessness begin? Go, ten minutes.

Write about a place you haven't lived. Go, ten minutes.

Make a list of thirty things pertaining to place; i.e., boulevard, street, corner, gulley, canyon, arroyo.

Write another ten minutes including ten words from your list but with this topic: the place I am most afraid to go.

Notice the different levels you can write about place. One is concrete: Colorado Springs, Colorado; Memphis, Tennessee; East Ninety-first Street near Kings Highway in Brooklyn, New York; Royce Road in Allston, Massachusetts; Monarch Drive in Sterling, Virginia; the Grand Canyon; Stinson Beach in Northern California.

The other is inner: I have not been in a peaceful place for a long time. I have been in a thoughtful place. I feel lost; I can't find a place for myself.

If you write only about the concrete—the trees and boulevards of Cleveland—it becomes dull, like dead cardboard. If you write only about your inner place—I felt sad and anxious and thought about nothing—the reader gets bored and disconnected. Anchor your inner world with details from the outer. And anchor the outer in a human life of feelings, hopes, desires, loves, and hates. Weave the two together. Integrate them.

Write about place including the two levels. Go. Ten minutes.

Some Place

We all come from someplace. Where do you come from? How did you escape? Go for ten.

Two

Often we are pulled between two places. They can be where you were brought up versus where you live now; a country place versus a city place; the sea versus the plains. What are the two places that pull at you? (Of course, there might be more, but for right now distill it to two.) Often they are projections of our inner psyche.

Go. Ten minutes. Tell us about them. Give us the pull, the conflict, the desire. Write.

No Topic

Having a topic to plow into can give your mind direction. You don't have to face the blank page without any tool.

But it's also healthy to have no topic and write into the wild unknown, with no markers, no direction, and see what comes up. Here you have to call to the center of your mind for help. In this way you build a spine in the middle of the vast empty dark and strengthen your ability to stand up in the unrelenting winds of change and shifting space. Have you noticed that even while you grab for the concrete it dissolves and one thought tumbles into another?

No topic is your attempt to grind out an existence, take a stand right in your lined—or unlined—notebook. It helps your immune system, but I can't tell you why. It's just so. Don't try to be logical here. To pay your bills, it's good to know how to count. Otherwise, put your shoulder to the fragile notebook and build a story out of nothing but lost memories.

Title

During a silent retreat, students did slow walking in a circle together outside in a drizzle. I suddenly remembered a poem by William Carlos Williams that I knew many years ago that seemed apropos to our week of practice. I recited it as close to verbatim as I could remember as we took one slow step after another.

> I have had my dream—like others—
> and it has come to nothing, so that
> I remain now carelessly
> with feet planted on the ground
> and look up at the sky—
> feeling my clothes about me,
> the weight of my body in my shoes,
> the rim of my hat, air passing in and out
> at my nose—and decide to dream no more.

When we returned to the meditation hall, I asked these twenty-five writing students, "What do you suppose the title to the poem is?"

They called out lines from the poem: "Had my dream," "Like others," "Dream no more," et cetera, et cetera.

"No," I said. "Would you like me to tell you the title?"

They nodded.

I paused, waiting for all of us to feel the weight of silence. "Thursday," I said.

They lit up. It was fresh, concrete, illuminating, surprising. His insight happened on an ordinary weekday. A Thursday. The best titles are like this.

Implied

Here's a section from "The Sea Is Not Full" by Katie Rauk:

> Hemingway asking the same ragged questions
> as he haunts dry creek beds. Stalks jack pines.
> Stares down the barrel of a shotgun.
> What's wrapped
> back in his drawer? What stubbed out
> sentences, what twisted spoons? And now
> his wife goes hauling the shotgun, too late,
> to the blacksmith shop. Demanding it be chopped
> into tiny pieces, a hundred if you can.

It is implied that the man shot himself. It's not necessary for Rauk to write: he blew out his brains. You can feel the suffering: "stubbed out sentences," "twisted spoons," the wife having the shotgun "chopped" up.

Implying things instead of stating them is a subtle art that takes time to learn. Pay attention when you read authors. See what is not stated and yet gives weight and throb to a piece. This does not mean hiding things or holding back a secret. It's more like: here is my open palm. We know but are not told: the other side has knuckles and fingernails. You don't need to say and explain everything.

Don't drown the reader; don't starve her either. It's a fine line to learn to walk.

Test VI

Three minutes on each of these topics:

____A lunch you loved

____A memory of a Popsicle

____A memory of sunscreen

____A memory of a doctor's appointment

Not Published

On a Tuesday and Saturday in July Garrison Keillor sat in his studio in St. Paul, Minnesota, and read two of my poems aloud on the *Writer's Almanac.* The first one he recited on public radio was "Top of My Lungs."

Even though I am unhappy
I come home singing at the top of my lungs
Shovel off the new snow and shove it on the old
Open the useless screened porch door
and take off my big boots
There are fried eggs
yellow as pearls
The old bed I dive into like a warm whale
The phone ringing
that duck on the wall
And even though I am unhappy
I sleep with the peace of flying angels
And even though I am sad
my wallet's empty
I buy the best soap
And even though my heart is hurting
out of sure will
I come home singing with the last night wind
and the first morning star
and the canary
and the summer that was killed below our house

I walk down to the Rainbow Café
call my Catholic friend Mary to come
have a drink and eat a turkey sandwich
The down coat I wear all winter still has the goose feathers
from a hundred flying birds
They let us smoke at our small table
Mary will always meet me here
They fill our glasses with the most sparkling water
for free
and the cold moon rises over the marquee
of the Suburban World theater
So even though I am unhappy
I throw back my old goat throat
and sing slowly
"Oh my darlin' Clementine"
by the beautiful lake in Minnesota
as the pressure of black night cold
moves in on us from all ten directions
I sing to the moon above the lake
"You are lost and gone forever"
calling the pure beast of loneliness down from the sky
with the old American song haunting city lights
"Dreadful sorry Clementine"
and though the very earth has swelled up
like an elephant with pain
I stand on its back singing
in this sad universe
where one lover leaves another for all time
and nothing to say with your feet on the ground

In 1981 I wrote it at the Croissant Express on Hennepin
Avenue across the Mississippi from St. Paul. Now twenty-five
years later it was being read where I wrote it. No one else but
a Minnesotan would know the exact Rainbow Café, now

gone, I referred to, or how winter curled your teeth and set you screaming. How fulfilled I felt so long after the writing of that poem. At the time I wrote it, I couldn't get it or any others published. I had a swath of them. My life was wholeheartedly dedicated to poems for more than a decade. I'd get a rejection and say to myself, I'm sure this is good, and shrug my shoulders.

Finally, at some point in disgust, and wanting to be part of the human race—I quit poems. I sat down and wrote a manuscript entitled *Writing Down the Bones*. From there on I galloped into prose. And here I was so many years later listening to my poem on the airwaves. I knew they were good, I said to myself again, but I was also long past the hard and wonderful journey into verse. I'd been writing prose for twenty years.

The point here is to go on. Don't get stuck with where you have not succeeded. Go on to something else. You don't know what will unfold. None of us has as much time as we think.

My mother used to say: Time waits for no man.

Ten years later you can look at your old manuscript and decide: Was it a dog or a jewel you had in your hands?

For now, let go. Go further. Stay connected to the power, the pleasure of writing. Come back to that over and over whether you get something published or not.

Too Long

What have you held onto too long? Go. Ten minutes.

Portrait

In the same way a painter does a portrait of a person, do a portrait in words of a person you know. Go, ten minutes.

As a writer, you can sketch not only the face you see, you can add what happened in the dark, what came to pass two years ago. You can draw in a third ear, a wart on the butt, three wishes they had and never fulfilled. Two ways they succeeded. In writing your portrait you have a great freedom. But also stay with that face, that body that you are drawing with language. It will help to ground the sketch. Keep coming back to something physical—the way your subject holds a glass or uses a toothpick.

Now let's drop the other shoe: do a self-portrait in the third person. Using third person for yourself helps you to unhinge from your sticky ideas of who you are. You may be surprised at the unattached truth you might discover.

Try doing a portrait of yourself in third person for five days in a row. Each day choose a different aspect of yourself for your portrait.

For example:

Day one: sports (so what if you never touched a ball—write that)
Day two: in relation to newspapers
Day three: in relation to September
Day four: in relation to Chinese restaurants
Day five: the thing she (which is you) would like to forget

Portrait

This is good practice in getting a different angle on yourself. We are multidimensional. Half of us holds Africa in our heart; another half eats cottage cheese.

Now forget about yourself altogether and describe someone you know dressing. Go, ten minutes.

Ad

Write a personal ad for yourself. You could write one you would imagine posting at thirty, at thirty-five, at forty. But to get warmed up, whatever age you are right now, write down a personal ad. Add a little about yourself, add some of what you want in a partner.

This is another way to get an angle on yourself. This could even be a separate chapter in your memoir—imagine coming upon it, placed discreetly in the perfect place, juxtaposed to a relevant chapter.

Allen Ginsberg wrote a personal ad that was published as a poem in a prominent magazine. His was a sincere call for love.

PERSONALS AD

"I will send a picture too
If you will send me one of you"
—R. Creeley

Poet professor in autumn years
seeks helpmate companion protector friend
young lover w/empty compassionate soul
exuberant spirit, straightforward handsome
athletic physique & boundless mind, courageous
warrior who may also like women & girls, no problem,

Ad

to share bed meditation apartment Lower East Side,
help inspire mankind conquer world anger & guilt,
empowered by Whitman Blake Rimbaud Ma Rainey &
       Vivaldi,
familiar respecting Art's primordial majesty, priapic care-
       free
playful harmless slave or master, mortally tender passing
       swift time,
photographer, musician, painter, poet, yuppie or
       scholar—
Find me here in New York alone with the Alone
going to lady psychiatrist who says Make time in your
       life
for someone you can call darling, honey, who holds you
       dear
can get excited & lay his head on your heart in peace.

                  October 8, 1987

At the end he put in an address:

        P.O.B. 582 Stuyvesant Station
        New York, NY 10009 U.S.A.

I'll tell you a secret: it was his real address. Everyone, of
course, thought it was a counterfeit.

I asked Allen if he got any response. "Only one or two," he
grimaced.

Last Letter

Write a last letter to someone. It could be someone you divorced, someone who died, someone you hate and will never speak to again. Say everything you need to say. This is it. You won't get another chance. Go.

You might imagine this letter as a separate chapter in your memoir.

Tell her about the gold wedding band, the way she ate ice cream, how you felt about her old age, the young image of her you carry in your mind, when her hair was pitch black, coarse, long, and curly. How much you wanted to be close and never knew how, instead rage rose in you like a metallic taste in your mouth. Tell her you'll miss her even though you never got along and never found a resting place with her.

You don't need to summarize or make a tidy ending. Many things go unresolved, have no closure. Allow truth, like an open bowl—don't try to put a lid on it or a bow.

One

If you could have only one memory, what would that be? Don't contemplate, muse, get dreamy, romantic. Dive in, let your hand flying across the page discover that single moment. Go, ten minutes.

And don't get cute and write "eating a coffee ice cream cone" and think you are done. I want to hear about the crunch of the cone, the color of the cream, where you were. It must be specific, not some general munching. One time, one place, one mouth, one hand that held it. Get going. I want it all.

Song

How about music? What songs do you love? What musicians? What instruments did you play? Tell us about practicing as a kid. What concerts have you gone to? Did you have a dream of being a rock star?

This is a whole dimension to explore. Music can be a memoir on its own. Your life with music. You don't need to be famous to write this. Just like writing about food or school, music is yours. It's playing for you right now. I can hear it. Begin with ten minutes—where is your favorite place to listen to music—and see where it takes you. Go.

Hattie's

Hattie's, named after Bob Dylan's song "The Lonesome Death of Hattie Carroll," is a bar on F Street in Salida, Colorado. The bar even has a subtitle, as though it were a book, "Shelter from the Storm," another Dylan title. The other unusual thing about the place is its long glass display case that usually would carry cigars but displays chocolates, the finest. Droste Pastilles, Toblerone, Ghirardelli, Lindt, Scharffen Berger, Cote d'Or, Valrhona, Green & Black's, Guylian. Serious chocolate, sixty percent cocoa, eighty percent, all lined up and stacked. The glass you peer through is crystal clean.

And on the actual bar, when you pull up a stool, are Ritter Sport bars: milk chocolate with rum, raisins, and hazelnuts, with praline, with marzipan. It changes the way you think of "bar." They do serve beer and wine and hard liquor and, if you want, they'll order out a pizza for you, delivered from across the street. In the afternoons they play classical music and at night Bob Dylan songs. Your glass of water has been filtered and to make ice cubes they filter the water twice.

While I sat writing at a booth—the only customer at eleven a.m.—a couple in tight jeans walked in and sat down nearby.

"We found your bar when we came here for the bikers rally a few weeks ago," the burly man with greasy hair told the owner.

The couple ordered iced tea and chips with salsa.

"I'm off for a week and I told my wife I'm driving down to Salida, wanna come?"

"Sure, I said," the wife chimed in. "Now we're here."

They drank their tea, ate their chips, and paid the bill.

"Now we can go home—drive the two hours—but it was worth it. She'll drive home." He pointed at his wife, standing near the front door.

"That's fine with me," she beamed. "It's a pretty drive."

They left and I kept writing.

The mountains surrounded the town, the clouds were high. I'd come here with a writing friend. We'd driven five hours north to do a writing retreat and got lost on the way. It poured; we had to cross a thin mountain pass. We rented a motel with two bedrooms and a kitchenette space with a couch. The first day I stayed back in the room and worked after taking a long walk around a lake with brown ducks squawking. Rob went to find a café to write in. We met at six for dinner.

The second day he came back at ten thirty in the morning after being gone since seven. He needed to use his computer and lugged up a card table he had borrowed from the office. He thought I was probably using the kitchen table. I thought it was getting crowded in there.

"I'm walking to town." I popped up. It was three blocks away.

I found Hattie's. Not a bad thing for a writer.

Bar

What bars have you known? Go, ten minutes.

Different Times

Tell me different times you needed chocolate or alcohol. Ten minutes. Go.

Broken

Stop a moment. What have you been broken about? This may take longer than ten minutes, but begin with ten. If you start to cry, keep your hand moving. If you have to pause to blow your nose—only this time—I'll say, okay. But get right back in there with your pen.

This is good—your heart is connected to your hand right now. Don't waste the opportunity. Get it down. You've felt sad and desolate many times in your life—this time take advantage of it. Move that pen. Don't be logical, explanatory. Let out whatever comes out the way it comes out.

Sometimes you have to be tough with yourself. It takes fortitude to transform your thoughts into something on the page. You can cry some more after you finish writing. For now keep going.

Everything

What do you know by heart? Go. Ten minutes.

Ache

What aches? First tell the concrete aches: your back, knee, toe, ear, wrist, head. How about stomach aches? When do you get them?

Now move to the other, less obvious injuries: heartache. Then how trees ache and trucks, how history, country, mountain, war ache. How bicycles ache, how roads ache, how you ache for a town and a sea, and how the sea and town also ache for you. How you know there is something else, somewhere else, someone else, how you also know it's right here and you can't touch it. How the very earth is groaning, reaching out to the sun. How all this desire and pain keep us going, revolving, twirling. You tell me about your aches; I'll tell you about mine. Go. Ten minutes.

The Topic of Topics

We can't recall one thing about going to church but then suddenly when you write about your mother's handbag, your whole religious scene becomes vivid.

Memory is not stored alphabetically in a file cabinet. Look behind you. Look in front of you. No memory. It's stored in your kneecaps, your toes, the space between your fingers, your teeth, nostrils, eyebrows. Your whole being experienced your life. Even if you weren't aware of it, your wrists, kidneys, back muscles were taking it in. How to seduce them to give up the goods?

Think of all the minutes and moments, days, seasons, months you have been alive. Even though your body is brilliant, it can't store all of that. The clouds and mountains, fields, rivers, wars, trees are also memory repositories. For help we have to call up oceans, tundras, glaciers, dried weeds, and old apples still hanging on branches.

We are not sure how to seduce all this immensity. That's why every foothold, angle, dimension of a topic is helpful. Ask yourself about kites, sandwiches, polo, Paris, rifles, Democrats, magnesium, the water table, tractors. But sometimes—and I want you to remember this—all these topics can sometimes make you foggy, spacey, ungrounded. Then it is time to come back to basics. I told you about these earlier, but here they are again:

I remember / I don't remember
I'm looking at / I'm not looking at
I'm thinking of / I'm not thinking of

When you have practiced these over and over you build a strong base. So when you shoot out too far, get disoriented in manufacturing ideas for writing, you can come back to the ABC's. Because you have practiced them, your cells will remember and you can call out in your muddle, *Yoo-hoo, Natalie, back to earth.*

Isn't it true in any sport? Though you teach your horse a lateral movement, or a transition between gaits, when the work is not going well you bring your stallion back to the simple practice on which the more advanced movements are built: stop, walk, stop, walk, stop, walk.

How good to have a foundation to come back to. Do not forget the basics.

More

I want to repeat two other basic exercises that I have mentioned before. I want you to reach for them when your writing feels lost.

This simple one: write what's in front of you. Nothing fancy. Begin by naming what you see: the plant leaning against the wall, the six panes of window glass, the electric socket on the wall . . . If your mind begins to recall something else, write that down too, but keep coming back to what's in front of your face. It is your anchor. Don't forget it.

The other one: Take a well-written book you love, open it, and read aloud (or silently) to yourself. Our minds are like radar. They zoom in and meet another mind, at whatever level it is functioning. If the writing you read is present, your mind mirrors it and also becomes present. If the writing is vague and meandering, your mind mirrors that too and becomes inattentive.

Let's look at this poem by Jack Gilbert, when he is at his highest moments of concentration. In the first lines don't try to understand what the fox is, just travel with it.

SEARCHING FOR PITTSBURGH

The fox pushes softly, blindly through me at night,
between the liver and the stomach. Comes to the heart
and hesitates. Considers and then goes around it.
Trying to escape the mildness of our violent world.

230

More

Goes deeper, searching for what remains of Pittsburgh
in me. The rusting mills sprawled gigantically
along three rivers. The authority of them.
The gritty alleys where we played every evening were
stained pink by the inferno always surging in the sky,
as though Christ and the Father were still fashioning
the Earth. Locomotives driving through the cold rain,
lordly and bestial in their strength. Massive water
flowing morning and night throughout a city
girded with ninety bridges. Sumptuous-shouldered,
sleek-thighed, obstinate and majestic, unquenchable.
All grip and flood, mighty sucking and deep-rooted grace.
A city of brick and tired wood. Ox and sovereign spirit.
Primitive Pittsburgh. Winter month after month telling
of death. The beauty forcing us as much as harshness.
Our spirits forged in that wilderness, our minds forged
by the heart. Making together a consequence of America.
The fox watched me build my Pittsburgh again and again.
In Paris afternoons on Buttes-Chaumont. On Greek islands
with their fields of stone. In beds with women, sometimes,
amid their gentleness. Now the fox will live in our ruined
house. My tomatoes grow ripe among weeds and the sound
of water. In this happy place my serious heart has made.

from *The Great Fires*

Now write for ten minutes, using the topic à la Gilbert,
Searching for _____, and you fill in the place.

How is this topic different from any we make up on the
spur of the moment? It is distilled from the grounded mind of
Jack Gilbert and we are charged by his focus.

Now you do it. Go. Ten minutes.

Cannot

What are the things that should never ever be said and right here you are going to say them? Go ahead. Bring yourself to say them. Ten minutes.

Radish

This is a wish: When you are writing about a radish, that you and the radish meet face to face. That you stay specific, present, and direct and through your true intention the radish becomes RADISH. You instantaneously summon the particular and also give life to the essence of that buried root plucked up red and edible. But don't try to be universal. That ends up being corny.

This wish is a hum, a blood vibration to know all things deeply, so that zinnia, too, is also ZINNIA. Z like in Zorro, slashing with your sword, your plucky pen, through the skin right into the cold hot bite of underground white that you throw into salad or stick your nose into the ruffled bright orange petal of that sprite zippy flower known to throw off bugs as good as garlic.

Listen to wishes like you listen to the wind. You don't think: what is it saying? You let the wind howl. That's all. Autumn will come, the night turn blue, the harvest over. Radish will grow grainy and zinnia will freeze. Someday you, too, will be gone. Nothing remains. Let your root and flower have an earnest intention and a light touch. Writing isn't writing. It's a flavor, a good reverie before you go to bed.

What wish do you have, that you hold and can also let go of? Go. Ten minutes.

Children

So, tell me, what was it like to have a daughter? How did it feel to have a son? Begin with a ten minute timed writing—even though you could write a book. Be honest. No clichés. What are their names?

In every workshop I teach there is at least one participant who lost a child. Write about that for ten minutes.

And those of you who never had one—how come? Tell us about that too. How did your life unfold? Go, ten minutes.

Flat Cake

Here's something obvious I never yet have gotten around to writing about: pancakes. Cooking them, eating them, blueberry, buckwheat, strawberry syrup, maple. In a café, in the kitchen. After making love, before going to sleep, at 3 a.m., for breakfast before school, on Sundays.

Go for ten minutes. Write about them for me, will you?

Orient Yourself

What is your essential anchor or orientation? The thing you come back to to know who you are? I asked this of a class in Santa Fe.

We had just gone on a lush walk, middle September, auspicious water trickling through an arroyo from a late night late summer storm. The plant world was alive. Flowering chamisa, purple asters, and wind. A kind of wind you didn't mind. It had its part and you welcomed it.

I said not to think, just say what comes to you.

Students immediately popped up with responses.

One said, ocean; another, pine forest; another, the life of work, also fast cars and thin lips.

I said for me it's loneliness and food. When that black dog of solitude is licking at my heels, when I call it to heel at my knee, I know I am close to home, my hand is down under some root—who are we, where does this end? Where will I be when death comes? Then I know my writing is my writing and no one else's.

But here's the catch: if I do not throw in some food—a cruller, a bun, a hamantasch—I become too serious, too tormented. It is food—come to the table right now—that softens the blow, makes living livable. So I am a two-fisted fighter. I shoot from the hip out of a double barrel. Bread and emptiness, a carrot and a vacuum, loss and a croissant. Cross my heart, cross my threshold, and you'll be blasted both ways.

What is your ground? What flashes across your mind without

thinking? Something odd?—fishing? photography? animals? sidewalks? Those aren't odd.

Stay with concrete nouns. Trust, honor, patriotism are too big words. Go under them, below them to something concrete. What do you trust? Bing cherries, clouds, butter.

These anchors can help you in writing. They are your language, the way you explain your universe. Whenever you get too lost, too far away, you can reel yourself in with what you know.

If you feel "ocean" is your answer, enrich your knowledge of it. Learn about tides, seaweed, salt, so when you pull in your anchor, you have rich material to troll from.

Yes, you are allowed more than one place you land. Of course, we probably have many. But don't scatter yourself. Land on a few and keep them close.

America feeds the idea that we can be everything, that there are many possibilities. That is true, but that idea can also make you crazy. It doesn't mean you can't change, but if you were brought up in Florida, in Georgia, in Idaho, you know some things naturally about those places. Don't deny it. Use it—and build from there.

Anchor

Tell me: what is your anchor, what you trust and know and can come home to over and over in your writing? Go. Ten minutes.

Inventory of Good-bye

Over a lifetime we've said good-bye in all sorts of ways: good-bye, I'll see you later; good-bye forever. Casual leavings and eternal departures.

Pay attention to the different kinds that happen each day. Let them roll around in your mind. Make an inventory or list of good-bys in your notebook. Wake up to the phenomena of separation. We come together; then we part company.

Notice the edge and poignancy of farewell and letting go. Both coming and going are important, but for a while look at the loaded situation, the dark experience of leaving. You've learned that detail is important but detail devoid of feeling is a marble rolling across a hard wood floor. The reason we want to write memoir is an ache, a longing, a passing of time that we feel all too strongly. If you want to recount your naval adventures, and it's a list of ships, positions, dates, time, it will be a nice record. But it will only be for you. It is not truly memoir.

The thing that is hard about good-bys is that often there is no resolution. There is no sense to death either. Well, sure they died, but when are they coming back? Never? How is that possible? I forgot to tell them something.

As a writer, you need to sniff out the snarls, the twists, the unsolvable situations. When you recall your father's two-day stubble, his cheap pipe, his long jowls, thick hands, and short neck, it is beyond judgment. It was someone you were full of feeling for—the details are imbued. He is no longer.

But none of this is negative. You are standing on a corner in a northern city waiting for a bus in January and the smell of a peony cuts through your mind, a glimmer of light, warmth, soft color and you are ready to fall to your knees. Summer and summer and summer rush upon you. Memory comes in the present gushing with feeling. Writing your memoir is a big yes.

Now back to particulars: list an inventory of good-byes, every time you can recall that you said good bye. Not general, make your list specific:

> Saying good-bye to my mother this July in Florida
> Good-bye to Mr. Clemente on the phone in 1989—he was on Long Island; I was in New Mexico.
> Good night to Ann last night sitting in the car. She kept on the headlights till I reached the front door.
> Hugging Sandy and Louise in the rain under an alcove on San Francisco Street after having dinner together
> Slamming down the phone on a solicitor

Add to it over time. This will perk your awareness and curiosity.

Even though you are keeping a list, for the heck of it: do ten minutes right now. All the times you remember saying good-bye. Go. Ten minutes.

First Meetings

Ten minutes: all the first meetings you've ever had, with a lover, a janitor, a teacher, friend, lawyer, owner of a shop, derelict, or a barber. Go.

Morning Glory!

Basho, the great Japanese haiku writer, wrote:

> Morning Glory!
> Another thing
> I will never know

Notice the exclamation mark after morning glory. He halted in his tracks in front of those electric-blue, paper-thin, almost transparent petals opening like a siren call. Usually there are hundreds on a vine. Basho zoomed in on a single one. The heart stopped—the limit of one's human life on earth. Here this flower, immense, glorious, impermanent, will be another thing he will never grasp or hold. With the force of his spirit, he calls out: "Morning Glory!" He is called to attention. And then the realization: this too I must let go of.

This is the way you should pounce. With one shout. Yes and no. I want. I will never have. All the places to travel, all the people to kiss and love, countries, mountains, books, foods you will never taste. The electric wire we walk, the choices we make and don't make, the days that are gone to us. We make our path through this tremulous life.

And then there are some things we do get to know. And then we get to say good-bye to them.

Go, ten minutes, what is there you will never know?

Give Up

What will you have to give up when you die? Go. Ten minutes.

Haunt

What ghosts haunt you? Write for ten minutes.

Divorce

Tell about a divorce. Go. Ten minutes.

Repeat

What did you start over again? Ten minutes.

One Thing

Here's a question: what is it mine to do? Not actively, but in the clear sense that a rock is a rock, a bird is a bird. We can go a little further: a refrigerator is not a stove. An apple is only and completely an apple and not a pear. And not even a shoe thinks to be something else. So what are you? What are you in your very core, irrefutable, in that part that understands that what you are is what you are? Thirty-one years full-time employment in a government office in Kansas City. Saturdays you visit your mother; Sundays you go for a long walk. And now you retire. Tell me what you are without complaint.

Maybe there is pain. You can feel the pain, but suffering is when you want it to be different, when you want to be a horse instead of a donkey, an éclair instead of a slice of bread. Suffering is when you want the pain to stop. Tell me what sycamore bombasts winter for its cold. Only human beings can imagine things to be different. Imagination creates books, but to write a good one you must accept things as they are. Don't run ahead of yourself. Let the breakup between lovers be that. The readers can lament. You, the writer, must stay at the root of all things: first thoughts, first feelings, first taste, smell, sound, before you want things to be different, before you decide you can't bear it.

So it is good to know what it is that is yours to do? The first question. To begin from there and then you can move out into the center of everyone's pain without trying to manipulate or make it different.

Plant this question inside yourself. You don't need to write anything for now. Let the question be like taste, flavoring your day. Don't expect one perfect, resonant answer. Stay in the inquiry. It will keep you open as you mow through your memories.

Hot

Where is the hottest place you've ever been? Ten minutes. Go.

What did your father never stop talking about? Ten minutes. Go.

What do these two topics have to do with each other? Probably nothing. But I don't want your mind to get lazy, comfortable in one slot. Slam dunk. One point. Now make another. We want surprise, not logic—in basketball and in writing. Do not be sensible. You'll never get out on the court.

Nothing

Stop, be useless, don't resist the states of mind you think are unproductive. In the depths of your sleepy, lazy, daydreaming self, in the parts you cut off, you can actually discover the source of your writing. This is good advice for all writers—for all human beings. Take some time to be unproductive, to let life go on without us.

This is true practice: To run in order to run. Not to get ready for a marathon or to look good in a bikini or to develop lung capacity. To write just to write is what writing practice is all about. To feel your hand move pen across the page. Pure joy—or pure sorrow—may arise but that is beside the point. To be empty of intention—even for twenty minutes—will provide much freedom and space.

Only then might you remember the root of all memory: the here and the now. Where else could memory possibly exist? Did you leave it back in the gas station when you filled your tank? Or in the shower under the soap? Memory only arises in the present.

Practice for no reason. Then all poetry, literature, even home, that evasive place, will come to you.

Winter

Write down the details of a funeral you attended in winter. Go. Ten minutes.

No Fun

This is the funny thing about writing memoir: we go back to retrieve our lives, to make sense of them. Often it is painful: to realize our mistakes, the wrong turns we made. But something else also happens. We come into closer relation with ourselves and have compassion for our bungling.

If you come to detest yourself through writing you are doing something wrong, cutting off the ability or desire to continue. My guess is you are pushing too hard, are too tough. Stop trying. This is not a race. Slow down.

Show me the person who hasn't royally goofed. Let's be honest, who hasn't lied, betrayed, disappointed? It is part of human life. Not a great part, but it is true. If we live fifty, sixty, seventy years—even ten—that's a lot of time. Many mistakes happen. No one hops on a palomino and gallops straight from birth to death. It doesn't even sound like fun. Lousy jobs, lousy lovers, lewd thoughts are the stuff of writing.

Hold this thought: "I came to love my life." Now discover its truth. It may take awhile but you can do it.

Mawi Asgedom in his memoir *Of Beetles and Angels,* about his family's escape first from war in Ethiopia, then from a refugee camp in the Sudan, writes:

> *Believe it or not, you will miss even the bullets and the cruel math teachers. For even the most horrifying memories are you; they are yours and no one else's. And they, along with the good memories, are your life.*

Trip

Often when I hike I think, oh my students would love this place. Then I'm taken up with how to transport them to this particular spot, what the writing assignment would be, and a reminder for them to drink water—this is desert after all. I rarely seem to have the pleasure of a hike all for myself—in my mind my students accompany me. This phantom development of curriculum has gone on for many years.

Finally this August I took the leap. I brought a caravan of twenty-five students in seven cars from Taos over to Abiquiu, New Mexico, where Georgia O'Keeffe lived. We left early in the morning after packing brown bag lunches. We passed over the Gorge Bridge spanning high up over the determined Rio Grande. I had the students pull over and do slow walking. We felt the almost imperceptible swaying of the bridge. Knees and stomachs twittered when looking down from such a height. These were people from Kansas City, Milwaukee, New York, Florida, Delaware, Canada. New Mexico was stark, bare hills all around, filled with sage.

We continued for a full two hours through country at the peak of summer. Cottonwoods, emerald green; Russian olive, swaying in sage color. We stopped at Bode's, a rural general store across from the great artist's house, for a quick bathroom break. Everyone piled out and rushed in. I couldn't get them back in the cars. They were shopping. For what? Horse harnesses? Campfire stoves? A fishing rod? Animal feed? It was something familiar: a cash register, candy, Coke.

I herded them back on our journey. We passed the Pedernal, a flat-topped mountain that O'Keeffe painted many times. She said she'd made a bargain with God. If she painted it enough it would be hers. Her ashes are buried on topof it.

We passed Abiquiu Dam and sheer pink cliffs, turning onto a dirt road to Ghost Ranch. Getting out of our cars, we stepped along an arroyo with little shelter. The sun beat down; the land was remote, vast, empty. We lunched under an elm and swam— some of us—in a murky pond. The rest looked on in dull wonder—very hot.

We wrote and sat on the bare ground, stopping after several hours at the Ghost Ranch gift shop. A frenzy of purchases ensued—new T-shirts, more candy, postcards, amulets, fetishes. And then we took the long drive back.

By evening I was informed that it was too long, they wanted to stay in the classroom. No more tedious exotic trips.

Right then I was differentiated from my students. They wanted to read about where I'd been but they did not necessarily want to go there. I was freed to hike alone.

I understood something else. They did not have to go to my wilderness to write, but they had to be willing to enter their own.

Where will you have to go, to tell your story? What desert will you have to enter? Go. Ten minutes.

Defeat

Tell me about a situation where you have been thoroughly defeated, where you arrived at zero, no hope. Don't justify, blame, or be ashamed. It just is as you just are. A place in you that never won, never conquered, never got it right. Tell me about that. Go. Ten minutes.

Sound

What do you hear? Throw in actual sounds that arise from your environment as you write. Go for ten minutes.

What are you afraid to hear? Go for another ten.

I hear my father in the night in his grave farther away than Manhattan. Like an oyster in his shell, my father is growing his other self six feet under. Once I threw in dirt over the coffin and heard it hit the hard wood. How did I ever let it happen? Let him go way into that redundant sta-tionary place? You know how old lettuce in the refrigerator bin turns into green liquid in a plastic bag? That's what happened to my father. Seven years now he is gone. We would have thrown out the lettuce long ago.

All these years it's taken to see I will never hear his voice again. He was a terrible father but there was enough there to love. You want details? Read my last book. There aren't any details anymore. There's no him, can't talk to him in the dark. He's on the mountain; in a star, a cloud, an old thrown-away shoe. Who am I who had a father? Where is the daughter, the girl?

A black river, a city cannot be forgotten. Tonight I am that man who was my father and I am the one heading for death and I am the one who sits with a wild joy like one white stripe on the back of a skunk. Does the moon have another name besides moon? Sun has only sun, sky has only sky and I, I had only one man who was my father evermore.

Go ahead. What sound are you afraid of? Ten minutes.

October Thirty-first

Over the years what Halloween costumes have you worn? Go.
Ten minutes.

Test VII

Three minutes:

_____A memory of watermelon

_____A memory of your favorite singer

_____A time you used crayons

Good

Here's a good and bellowing memoir: *Waiting for Snow in Havana* by Carlos Eire. The subtitle is *Confessions of a Cuban Boy.* Not everyone declares (or calls it) "memoir." Eire could have subtitled it "rant" if he wanted to.

Here's another fine and subtle memoir: *The Black Notebooks* by Toi Derricote. Her subtitle: *An Interior Journey.* Another way of looking at the close examination of a life.

Yesterday in the bookstore I saw a new nonfiction book by Jonathan Franzen: *The Discomfort Zone.* His subtitle was *A Personal History.* It, too, was shelved under memoir.

Each writer has his slant, "confession," "interior journey," "personal history," his way of making the word "memoir" closer to his skin.

Think about this. What will you subtitle yours? Make a list and play around with it. You have time to come up with the right one. It will come to you as you write, but it's good to plant a seed. Nothing grows without one.

Big State

Tell me all you know about Texas. But you lived in Oregon. Write about Texas anyway. It can have a boomerang effect and shoot you deeper into your knowledge of Chicago or Evanston.

And you can also begin with: "I don't want to write about Texas, what I want to write about is" and go directly into writing about your state. But do you see? This little rebellion plunges you deeper than if I simply said: "Write about the state you were brought up in." A topic phrased like that only calls up grammar school compositions that you hated.

Now, resisting or not, go. Ten minutes. Give me Texas.

The Big Continent

Tell me about the time you went to Africa. You never went?
What were you doing instead? Tying your shoes? Eating a hamburger? Riding the bus downtown? Reading about Kenya in the
library? Whether you went or not, Africa is offering a great
writing opportunity. Go. Ten minutes.

Poignancy

Where did you always want to go but didn't? Writing about the places we didn't go sometimes gives even more poignancy to our writing. Write for ten minutes.

What

What did you sincerely learn from your father? Go. Ten minutes.

Orchard

At a celebration for the twentieth anniversary of my first book, a woman who studied with me when she was twelve and thirteen back in the middle seventies stood up to speak.

"At a hippie school in Taos, New Mexico, named Da Nahazli, meaning *Spring Will Come Again* in Navajo, one Monday Natalie brought in a bushel of rich red apples she'd picked the day before at an orchard in nearby Ranchos. This was a family orchard where a month before the oldest son aged thirteen had been buried. He was shot in a bizarre gun accident. That young man had been my first love."

She explained that though we all thought we were very hip and open we actually had no avenues for expressing grief or any skills to help this young girl make sense of what had happened.

She described how I handed out the apples to the eleven students—and told them the apples came from the Zimmermans' and said, Eat them and while you do, trust yourself and write everything that comes to mind. You have a full hour.

She said that that morning she was given the avenue to freedom, the tool to make sense of her suffering, the long path of writing she has continued for more than thirty-five years.

I'd like to tell you I understood the significance for her of what I did that early winter morning, but I didn't make that large connection in my mind between the apples, Philip's death, and first love.

Instead, I was hell-bent on this electric, new way of writing. I was dancing with it. I wanted these scraggly kids in this hogan out back of the main building to drink it down like Kool-Aid, like the true charged vitamin C.

I see now at least one of them entered the river of its significance and understood the importance of continuing.

This is to tell you one of the jobs of writing: to not pass over hurt, loss, missed connections. It is not to wallow but it is to recognize and acknowledge all the humps and turns and to carry grief. And while nations plunge on to more wars and unforgivable destruction in the name of defense, then sign breakable treaties, and new dictators rise to power and even democracies betray themselves, a writer does not forget, does not get lost in the chaos, but remains with the howls, the outrage until they are honored and spoken of.

This might seem a great leap from a young girl and an apple orchard to political chaos and global suffering, but it is not. A human being begins in the personal and must stay in the personal to survive. Sweeping generalizations is what lets hundreds of thousands of people be killed.

It's a holy thing to be a writer. It is why you want to write your memoir: to remember all of it. The good and the bad. To trust your experience, to have a confidence that your moments and the moments of others on this earth mattered, not to be forgotten, wiped out with the new decree, the better plan.

It is a great thing you are doing whatever it is you are remembering. You are saying that life—and its passing—have true value.

Right now before you have time to think: what can you celebrate? Go, ten minutes.

Mother

Tell me about your mother's hands. Go. Ten minutes.

Resistance

Always just before you pick up the pen, no matter how much you look forward to writing—or don't—a ball of resistance, like a gathering of yarn, coalesces in the center of your desire. It puts up a red flag, stop, no, I can't. A big gruff umph, I don't want to. No matter how many long years you have written, no matter how much success and praise you've received, it doesn't mean a thing. The test continues, do we really have to, haven't I done enough? It's human nature, this question, this tug to stop.

We want to hear a simple remedy: pay no attention, charge ahead and write.

But how about a slightly different tactic: greet the resistance, honor its significance, give it a nod. Below its brief red flag is your finest opponent: inertia. It's saying, leave well enough alone, don't make waves, don't cause trouble, don't speak, don't step forward. Let the world roll over you.

This time you can afford the grace to be cordial. The pen is in your hand. Howdy-do, you salute your formidable foe. No need to be fearful. You have your tools. You know the territory and you know your job. Now with a deep out-breath of air, dive into the center of your mind, plunge far out into the Atlantic where no lifeguard can stop you. You can't even hear the horn or whistle. You are enfolded in the lapping sea.

Knew

What did you know that you didn't want to know. Go. Ten minutes.

Air Waves

Tell me everything you remember about a radio. Was there a
special show or announcer you listened to? Go. Ten minutes.

Cracked Sentence

The sentence, that unit of language we speak and write with can be charged, the muscles in its arm can have definition, packing a wallop. "Now a stoic ice radiates within me." See the juxtaposition of cold ("ice") and hot ("radiates"). It burns off your eyebrows.

How about this: " . . . And also, it was an afternoon in September when . . . I sowed, in your living coals, the pools of this night in December." Bounces you around into time, heat, water, the dark side of day and winter all in one line.

"Summer, now I'm going away. The meek little hands of your afternoons pain me." Here, something inanimate is being addressed. Why don't you address a bench, the sun, a leg, grape, flannel skirt, night, Houston?

All these quotes are from poems by the Latin American poet César Vallejo. Sometimes we are compelled to go to the poets to learn how to make our writing flash.

You can crack open sentences, like egg shells letting the bright yellow, the clear white, in all its unorderliness, fall out. Memoir is about breaking structure, slashing through thoughts and the old way things were held. Know that the subject in the right place might be cumbersome, that the object might carry the true heart. Scramble up your language. Let intestines be a string of emeralds, worship brides and degenerates. Don't believe history. Find another chronicle. Discover a new math. Cradle a car engine.

The Japanese don't say, I see the dog. Their structure translates to, I dog seeing. While you are looking at Fido, the canine is also looking at you. As you hike through the woods the pines might be naming you and the mountain might see your future—it's not a pretty one, the girl with the pearl earrings will stop loving you.

No memoir is complete without hunting down the leopard, but when you turn in the pampas grass, acacias all around, you are surrounded by cheetahs—you are already in one's jaw.

Now what do you do? Step inside the unknown.

Clocks can spin your grandmother right out of the grave. Don't believe a bakery is closed. Shout through the door for them to open it again. Don't try to be profound; try to understand things deeply. What you need is before you. Your memories are in your back pocket. Settle down into the unstructured universe. Look around you. Are the clouds marching in unison across the sky? Are rocks a standard size?

Write in the organic midst of the disarray. The vultures will cheer you as they circle overhead. You are not dead meat yet, but they'll love you anyway. So will the tenement stoop, the delivery truck making a wrong turn, the broken neon pizza sign. With all this encouragement you can't lose.

When I drive home from leading a five-day retreat, I sometimes think all I do is drag my students into their suffering. They want to be happy. So do I. But real joy includes agony. If your writing is weighed down too heavily on the side of happiness it is lopsided, missing the picture, and I hate to say it, like a commercial, how a detergent will wash everything clean. It's the stains that catch the eye, the odd turn of her nose that makes us fall to our knees. Good looking is overrated. Perfection is a false dream. Write about the man shoving fries in his mouth with greasy long hair, buck teeth, a ring in his nose, frayed jeans he trips over that are about to fall off. Already you can see the crack in his ass when he bends over.

Make your memoir pretty and no one will read it.

Down

What was the great burden you carried? Did you ever lay it down? Go for ten.

Test VIII

Three minutes on each of these topics:

____A time you were freezing in July

____A memory of leaves turning

____A time you planned a trip and didn't go

Series

Write a series of postcards to someone. Each postcard can be a paragraph. Postcards are sent from different places, creating different slants of mind, different details.

Juxtapose them on a page or make them a whole chapter of your memoir. The postcard from the plaza, the one from the curb, the car mechanic's, the laundry. Or you might have lived an international life: one from Colombia, Hong Kong, Yugoslavia, Berlin. I'll tell you a secret—you don't have to go to these places to write one from there. But remember this is memoir. You can't lie. "If I was in Paris this is what I'd write you: I'm eating croissants like they were going out of style. I'm sick of looking svelte for you. I'm hungry and I'm finally going to eat. And not just food. I'm taking in gardens, books, fountains, cobblestone. And I intend to lick the first Cezanne I see. Yours, Molly."

Fulfilled

The author Willa Cather believed that if you had a wish for something from a young age—for example, being an opera singer—and you continually made effort at it, you would live a fulfilled life. It didn't matter if you were on stage at the Metropolitan; maybe you sang in a local theater; perhaps you took lessons and belted it out in the shower and at family gatherings. That was good enough. The important thing was to stay connected with your dream and that effort would result in a basic happiness.

Cather said that those who gave up carried something painful, cut off inside, and that their lives had a sense of incompleteness.

In the same way a haunted feeling surrounds writers who have written one successful book then disappeared. What happened? we wonder. Even if their second or third were not half as good, never lived up to their first, we feel the lifeblood is still flowing. We sense something dead, abandoned, hollow—where is their soul?—of the one-book writer.

So what a victory it was when Henry Roth, after his disappearance for decades after *Call It Sleep* came out, published more books more than thirty years later. He'd been working anonymous jobs in New York, Providence, then Boston, descending into ever deepening silence. He finally burrowed into Maine, killing geese for a living, and raising two sons, but something finally kicked in. Such joy and exhilaration. Henry, you're back.

We love a good book but we sense there is something more—a good and vital life.

Don't let the light go out. Get to work, even if the going is slow and you have six mouths to feed and two jobs.

A few years ago I was invited to meet with the creative writing students in a graduate program at a big midwestern university. When I asked what their plans were, eight out of the ten, turning up their empty palms, said, well, the most we can hope for is a job at a community college. We know it's hard out there in the book world.

I was quiet and looked down. In their heart of hearts I wanted them to be thinking: Tolstoy, Garcia Lorca, Jane Austen, Proust, Alice Walker, Naguib Mahfouz, Virginia Woolf, Chinua Achebe. They seemed beaten-down, too practical, too rational at such young ages. All of them should have been hungry to step up to the plate and smack the ball home. What happened?

Great writers do not write so that their readers will feel defeated. They wait for us to blow on the embers and keep the heat going. It is our responsibility. When we understand this, we grow up. We become a woman. We become a man.

No institution can give you this authority; though you may learn many wonderful things there. Like a little bird, you must open your small beak and feed yourself one drop of rosewater at a time, then a kernel of corn, a single sesame seed, even a tiny pebble. Keep nourishing yourself on great writers. You will grow from the inside out and stand up on the page.

No protest, no whining. Right now take a nibble of bread. Make a bit of effort. It does not have to be enormous. Just go in the right direction and the trees, insects, clouds, bricks of buildings will make a minute turning with you and salute you.

Test IX

Three minutes on each of these topics:

____A pair of shoes that hurt your feet

____A memory of reading something in the newspaper that broke you in two

____A time you had a toothache

____Something about insects: crickets, ants, spiders, yellow jackets, a dragonfly, fleas, praying mantis, ladybug, beetle

____Better do another one on bugs. There are a lot of them.

Baby Memoir

You may not want to write a full book on a great tomato, a cow, how President Bush affected your life, the three short times Hemingway lived in your Kansas City. Ten pages will do. Or three, two, fifteen.

Unfortunately, the word "essay" usually gets a bad rap in our society. *"Hand your essays in by Friday." "You must write a five-hundred-word essay on the American flag."* As adults we hear the e-word and flee, but in truth essays are a delectable form and have the potential to be a baby memoir—fresh, alert, compact, rather perfect. They are short invitations to come along with the writer as she excavates a memory or rolls around in a nuanced thought. As the picture unfolds, the reader can be there in an organic way.

You won't live long enough to write a whole book on every topic you deem suitable. But here you have an alternative. Roll out the toddler memoir. In a few pages you can make your father's teeth, the A-bomb, traffic on the L. A. Expressway, or a bad haircut sizzle. An essay can be so strong and concise that it rises up three dimensional and you can walk around it.

Choose a meaty subject right now, one that you can bite into and chew—not for too long—but long enough to digest. And write about it.

You can begin writing about the topic in five ten-minute spurts or a one-hour nonstop writing. Then leave those pages until the next day or three days or a week. Reread what you have. Chop it up, take only what glares back at you, has vitality.

Keep those pages. List other things you want to include. Often an essay is built on a few seemingly dissimilar events, people, places, things.

Write again. Repeat the process. Do you see: you are writing about two days when you thought you might have had cancer. For some reason, a canoe trip in Utah, cooking blueberry pancakes for breakfast, persists in your mind. Instead of throwing it out, see if you can fold it in. Everything doesn't necessarily have to blend. Nuts and raisins add moments of contrast or intensify the main flavor.

Keep kneading and making your bread. Write, leave it for awhile. Come back.

Nothing is as exquisite as a good essay. Don't listen to stout Mrs. Post, your old English teacher. And you know how I honor teachers, but there is a time to take back the years you lost in high school. The time is now.

Caryl Phillips

Caryl Philips, a fine writer born in St. Kitts in the Caribbean, and brought up in Leeds, England, said, "It's not how much you want it, it's what you are prepared to give up."

Can you go without a little less sleep tonight?

House

Now what? All along while you did writing practice, you were forming your memoir. You realized you needed to write about the cottonwoods, that they played a big part in the way you fell in love with your first husband. At another point it was the magnolias, the azaleas, the crawfish étouffée that set love spinning when you were eight or nine and those stories about the Korean War you heard your parents whisper in the other room, they blackened your heart.

You write about all this. Themes begin to form and cluster. You add a little color here; some robins there. A highway, a juke joint, Robert Johnson's guitar, a bayou, a parish.

Keep writing. Keep filling out the story. Make a list of topics in the back of your notebook that you plan to write about. The more you open and pay attention, the more topics will come to you. Meeting your older brother in the hallway in the dark—you wrote it once. You didn't get it down right. Write it again over time, from different angles, different times of the day, from different feelings till you know, yes, you laid this one down. The memory rests.

But now what? How do you form it into a manuscript?

This is when you stop calling on the universe, stop surrendering, stop being submissive to everything. You've let it grow to a plump pile in front of you. This is when you become individual; you become accountable. You have to recognize your intention, your direction.

You don't get nitpicky; you don't get critical. You get exacting, merciless, direct. This goes; this stays. This writing about pudding belongs after the writing about being hit by a lawnmower. At sixteen you hear about Martin Luther King, Jr., then there is the story about the swans across the lake and how your father was going to run for governor, then King comes in again. Each topic can be a separate chapter, varying long and short, or you can mix all topics into sections of one chapter. You decide what is the most powerful.

You form this mass of writing into a breathing organism, into a possum, a raccoon, an alligator with egrets overhead.

You build your story. Without the material that is the writing, you'd have nothing to build with. It would be empty air, vacant hopes—oh, someday I'll write that book. Instead you have given a good long time to developing the memories, writing them down. You have honored them.

Once you have those materials, you construct your house. Some know right away how their manuscript will develop: into a split-level. Yours might be the shape of a hut, a hogan, an earth-ship. Or ranch-style. You may not be clear about what you want. Keep reading through what you have written. Take long walks and let the form develop in your belly, below discursive thinking. Maybe what you conceived as the last chapter should open the story.

I'm afraid you might have to write some more. I'm afraid you might have to throw out pieces that don't belong.

Have a tantrum if you need to. Decide writing is a lonely, boring, selfish act and plan to leave it. Then don't. Stay in the process. Get your arms around it.

You gave your wild mind a lot of galloping room. Now you need to pick up the reins and direct it to trot down a path, your path. You can't take the whole wheat field with you but you can canter through it and say you were here. Go ahead. You grew the wheat, now cut it down, make your own shadow line through the yellow stalks. Don't worry. The wheat is golden, waiting for this moment.

Recipe

Some memoirs have a relevant food recipe at the end of each chapter. Let's take it from another angle:

What is the recipe to shop for clothes?

The recipe to get along with your spouse.

Write down the ingredients and the steps of preparation with no commentary.

Give me the recipe to brush your teeth.

To keep up with the daily news.

What is the recipe to make a rock? A wolf?

Get the idea? Hit the ingredients on the nail and you have an unusual chapter and way of telling something.

Make your memoir rich with ingredients. Not with big ideas but with one thing after another. A recipe or meal is a chapter, then a letter is another chapter, then a succinct memory. Brick by brick. Just like you cook a meal: you don't stir in the mashed potatoes with the Jell-O and pour it over the steak. Each component is separate, has its own integrity. But it all comes together as dinner. The same with the chapters of your book.

Diet

Julia Cameron, author of *The Artist's Way,* wrote a book called *The Writing Diet.* What a delightful idea.

If she asked me for a recipe, this is what I'd give her:

Ingredients:
clear glass
water

Directions:
Put water in glass and take long drink.

Purpose:
The writer's mind needs to be transparent, clear, objective, unbiased.

Maybe I'd add:

Optional:
a squeeze of lemon

Even better, add in a dash of cayenne. Something surprising. Sit up in your seat. Get alert. Come to attention.

This is a good recipe, don't you think? Nonfattening, quenches thirst, the main ingredient can still be found for free.

Too much coffee makes the nerves quack. Too much cake, you become sluggish, pudgy.

On the point: water. Take a gulp, meet the next hour.

Question: What recipe would you offer for Julia Cameron's book?

What does a writer have to eat? Go. Ten minutes.

Structure

I could tell you what water is made of: two parts hydrogen, one of oxygen. I could describe what it feels like to dive into a lake on a hot summer day or the briny feel of sand and salt at the beach, but the task here is to find your own pool of liquid and give it shape. How do we form our writing into a structure, a book?

A part of me wants to say simply I don't know, and I don't mean this flippantly. I am saying structure is yours to discover. You have to find your own dynamic structure, one that fits your story and what you personally have to share. Ultimately, that's what you will need to do, but we need examples, ways that other people structured memories, a portion of them, into a cohesive whole.

The key here is *organic,* finding the way that is natural to what you have to write, like the course a river cuts to let its water flow. This might sound *oh so lovely*—sitting beside the fat wide muddy Mississippi with a glass of mint julep—but some rivers—like the Middle Fork of the Salmon in Idaho or parts of the Rogue in Oregon—have rough white water and jagged death-defying spins and reverses. Authentic to your voice means finding a container shaped to hold it, not some preconceived form, but something true for what you are saying.

As we look for structure, it's helpful to remember what novelist William Faulkner said about plot: it's that "thin red line" that runs through the text. Plot is what makes you turn the page, makes you want to continue reading. I call that "red line" spine.

Get a strong spine and you have freedom of movement. Often shaped like an arc, it holds up and drives the story forward.

But I hesitate to use the word "story." When we hear that word we often have a tight idea of beginning, middle, and end. In memoir it's more the experiences, adventures, moments that form the structure. But reading one of Faulkner's books releases you from any worry about how taut and trim that line must be. If anything Faulkner leads you into a tangle. In any case, it's good to keep his suggestion in mind.

Let's look at some published memoirs now with the intent to specifically study structure:

Paul Zweig wrote a memoir, *Departures,* that went out of print before I could hound everyone to read it. There are three sections. The first two are each divided into nine short chapters. Each chapter seems to glide to the next one as though the number four or five delineaing them is simply a breath. I don't know if Zweig planned that both sections contained nine chapters, but think of it—that's an interesting structure to set up ahead of time and then fulfill.

The first two sections are about his twenties as a young poet in France, his sexual excursions, and his suffering because of them. These sections vibrate with sexual juice. "Michèle's physicalness was so powerful. When I entered her, she seemed to rush over me like a soft river; then she bit my chin, and I went wild."

But Zweig also turns this visceral energy to whatever he explores: his return visits home to Brighton Beach, to learning French:

And then something happened that was overwhelming, although curiously uneventful. I had no name for it. Little by little I began to make sense out of the French I heard in cafés and restaurants, on the radio, in fleeting conversations. Much of it I still didn't understand, but I began to notice that it was language, expressed by the voices of these people with tight lips who seemed to talk through me with spars and splinters of sound.

To the smell of cheese:

My sense of belonging was made up of the ammoniac smell of old Camembert, or better of Livarot cheese, which I learned to chew slowly, so that it barely slid over my taste buds, cut by thick Algerian wines. It was the smell of the horse-meat butchers in the building up the block. It was the acrid smell of Michèle's vagina, when it was wet and full of my come, a smell that frightened me, with its suggestion of marshes and peat bogs that were insatiable and ominously soft. It was the smell of thick coffee, and bitter black tea when we were sitting on the floor of our room discussing Lukacs. It was the smell of the perfume worn by Michèle's younger brother Lucien, which clung to the walls of our little hallway, lingering in the bathroom, full of arrogant eroticism, and Lucien swinging past us, his magnificent blond head falling into statuesque poses, as if by some genius of the blood.

Though both sections are about France, the second section is more reflective: his French experience rubbing against his Jewish childhood, his political awakening. He moves closer in the second section.

But all three sections are, as the title indicates, about departure. In the first two the departures are from his New York background and from the fact he was heading to college to become an engineer, took a 180-degree turn, became a poet, and moved to Europe. What compels us through the material, though, is not the "story" but the detailed, pumping writing itself. It explodes on the page. It's the red line that keeps the reader going.

The third section, much shorter, is another kind of departure. He is in his forties suffering from lymphoma and it is about his fight to stay alive. This section is nineteen pages long, one straight shot, no breakup into chapters, still full of exceptional vitality. As you read, you realize how extraordinary the structure of the book is—juxtaposed to death in the third section, we have the first two about youth and sex. What would you write about if you had a terminal disease? Life takes on a compelling dimension when you taste the brink of its transiency.

Underneath these obvious departures is the emotional one: Zweig is on the run, leaving, exiting, fleeing. He is a wandering Jew who never lands. Zweig might not have known he was expressing this constant decamping below the surface, but it is his inner truth revealed.

We do the best we can as writers, but often something gets exposed that we are not aware of about ourselves—a third thing, that is overriding, yet subtle, is mirrored out of the depths of our detail—this element is out of our control. The reader discovers it. It makes the writing more delicious, more dimensional, but it's also why, in the end, writing is a naked thing.

But for structure's sake let's reiterate: Zweig had three sections each dealing with different kinds of departure. "Departure" can be a big word and in the first parts Zweig gave himself much latitude and room for exploration. The departure, facing sickness and death, in the third created a driving structure, cut away anything else, made a strong trajectory. These three sections were the *physical structure* of the book.

The "thin red line," turning pages, came from the muscular, urgent detail. You'd follow Paul Zweig anywhere with this kind of alive writing. Remember: no one can give you this writing authority. You find it through practice.

Also note: mostly memoir doesn't have a whodunnit? element, but there are no hard and fast rules. The structure fits what you are building.

The physical structure of *The Language of Baklava* by Diana Abu-Jaber is twenty-four chapters. Each chapter has a heading, for example, "Hot Lunch" or "The First Meal," followed by writing pertaining to that topic, and then a coincident Middle Eastern recipe is given. (Ahead of time I asked the kitchen at the workshop where we read this book to cook some of the dishes for dinner. Eating the actual food added a whole new dimension, snap, crackle, pop, to the book. These were not obligatory recipes; these were essential bones of the structure.)

After the recipe appears there is a physical space and then often more writing, another new take on the same topic. The writing is intimate, revelatory, funny, given to insightful, zesty vignettes about her father, food, her Jordanian relatives, or her American mother.

Writing students take note: by now you should have hints from Abu-Jaber of how one might build a book. Choose a topic and then pour your heart out. A pause, another wave of recall. In Abu-Jaber's case, though, it seems the topic—or heading—was derived from what she first wrote and the heading came after the writing.

I loved the book while I read it, but when I put it down I was not pushed to pick it up again for several days, even a week. Consequently, it took me almost three months to read the whole thing. This is not always bad. Our society is too quick and speedy, but as a student of writing, I must ponder why I kept dropping the thin red line.

I asked the class if any of them had experienced a similar reaction. About two-thirds raised their hands.

We explored the idea that she wandered too far and should have stayed closer to the central themes of food and her father. We definitely were compelled to find out if he eventually got his own restaurant. This would have given the book a clearer direction. Maybe she tried to cover too much? She had written several successful novels so she knew about plot, about following that thin red line. Maybe with her own personal material she lost her way?

We were going on in this track when a student raised her hand. "Natalie, look at the last paragraph. She says, 'I am as surely a Bedouin as anyone who has traveled in a desert caravan. A reluctant Bedouin—I miss and I long for every place, every country, I have ever lived . . . '"

A turning like a kaleidoscope, a new perspective suddenly came into view: I had missed it. This structure was like a wandering Bedouin. She dropped down in one place, taking the water where there was a well, a spring, one or two trees, a course of memory to be followed. She lingered awhile, then picked up stakes and wandered somewhere else. Stopped again, fed her herd and her family, set up camp for a brief period.

"Oh," I said, seeing the dimension of the book extend over three months of my life where I picked it up and put it down like a Bedouin.

I don't know if Abu-Jaber was aware of the extraordinary structure she created. Sometimes we back into our form without knowing it, like working with a hum of insects in the background. If Abu-Jaber was totally aware of the structure it might have been too self-conscious—"I'll mirror the wanderings of a Bedouin"—yeah, right.

It's probably better as writers to know what we are up to but always—if the book is good—a third thing is revealed to the reader, often unknown to the writer. Isn't that the way life is, too?

House Made of Dawn by N. Scott Momaday is a novel, but there is a lot to learn from its *very* thin red line. He wrote it when he was studying poetry in the sixties for an MFA at the Stanford Creative Writing Program, started by the novelist Wallace Stegner.

Momaday saw that the fiction writers in the program were receiving all the attention. He thought, I can write a novel too—and, thus, this book, which won the Pulitzer in 1969. It is to the award committee's credit that they recognized it. It's a poet's novel about the Southwest and the mind of a Native American, connected to the land.

If you read it, take warning, do not race ahead to find out what happens. Something does happen, but what is front and center, what is the big character in this book is the earth and the slow movement of time. If you read page after page, you feel the red dirt, the big sky, you enter the rhythm of a dry place. Against this backdrop, one watches the slow plot, the suffering of an individual. Often what is not said has as much power as what is said.

Momaday broke a code in this book and found a true form to express a Native American's way of seeing. He opened the space for other Native American writers—Leslie Marmon Silko, James Welch, Sherman Alexie—to follow.

Maybe you, too, are writing about a place. Fully give us that place, but have the tension of a red line to bring us along. The direction doesn't have to hit us over the head, but we have to want to turn the page, not just lie down and sleep in the meadow you describe on page one. What is your pain against this backdrop of place? There must be a juxtaposition, a tension, a little trail of blood along the Beauty Way. Place by itself doesn't create trouble, even if your place is an urban street corner. It just is. It's when human beings enter that the tumult starts.

Momaday not only cracked open structure in this book to allow us to roam in a new field of the mind, but he also did something else. He wrote with such intimacy that structure melted away and no separation existed between you and the things written about. You are there and you feel it. Here is an example:

You went in and put your hands to the fire. Your grandfather scolded you and smiled, because you were little and he knew how you felt. He cut off a piece of mutton and put it down for you. You could smell the coffee and hear it boiling in the pot, even after he took it off the fire and poured it into the cups. You could see it, how black and hot it was, and there was a lot of smoke coming out of the cups. You had to let it set a while because the cups were made of enamel and they could burn your hands. It was hard to wait, because you were cold and you knew how good it was going to taste. But the meat cooled right away and you could pick it up and it made your fingers warm. The fat was full of juice and smoke, and sometimes there

was a little burned crust on it, hard black flakes that you could feel on your
teeth, and the meat was tough and good to chew. And after a while you
could pick up the cup and hold it in your hands. It was good just to hold
it. You could see the dull shine of it, where the grease from your fingers was,
and the black smoking coffee inside. And when you drank it, it was bet-
ter than the meat. You could feel it all good and hot and strong inside of
you, and the good hard grounds on your teeth and tongue.

House Made of Dawn.

The Road from Coorain by Jill Ker Conway is a more traditional memoir. Born at the beginning of the Depression, she was almost sixty when this book was published. Readers have a sense that this is a well-digested life. The back cover calls it an autobiography but the front cover says, " . . . clear-sighted memoir of growing up Australian." The structure follows chronology: her childhood on the western plains of New South Wales and her intellectual development as a young adult. What is so compelling is the depth of her examination of whatever she writes about. You are suddenly engrossed in shearing time on her family's sheep farm. Have I ever been interested in this before? Not particularly. But Ker Conway's clear authority, her knowing things thoroughly guides the reader along to new places and new pleasures.

Interwoven throughout the book is her relationship with her mother and her mother's slow breakdown—we watch it happen. And we want to know if, how, and when Jill will break free of it—this is the plot line. But any emotional truths that are revealed are clearly conscious to Ker Conway. The writer here is not out of control. Her direction is so strong that we barely notice the physical structure—nine sections of twenty to fifty pages each—that holds it up.

Ker Conway adheres to a linear structure. When you crack open structure, a new kind of energy is released. But the energy in *The Road from Coorain* has a straight trajectory. What we know, the author has discovered through obvious, earnest, hard work. Look at the first presentation of her mother:

By all accounts, my mother, always handsome, was then an extraordinary beauty. She was tall, slender, and graceful in carriage, and blessed with a coloring of skin and hair which made her memorable. Her abundant, curling hair was deep auburn highlighted with gold, but instead of the redhead's tender skin she had an olive complexion which tanned to a fine rosy color without a hint of a freckle.

The details are right there, laid out simply one after the other, but this does not mean the author is not later also allowed penetrating analysis:

After their departure my mother was in a high state of excitement. She kept on and on like a fugue demanding that I agree with her that her actions had been warranted. When I told her they weren't, that she had behaved unforgivably, the whole cycle was repeated again and again. It was after midnight before I could retreat to my study and assess the events of the day. Because the explosion had not been directed at me, I could see it more clearly for what it was. My mother was now an angry and vindictive woman, her rages out of all proportion to any real or imagined slight. She was most destructive toward her own children, especially where she had the power to damage their relationships with others.

Ker Conway has earned this analysis. Whenever she does an explication, we can come along with her, because she has first piled on concrete experience that we read about, so that anything she comes to understand, we can understand, too.

In *The Road from Coorain* each chapter—you can feel it—has been gone over and over and refined. But I'm sure it wasn't a nitpicky scratching out of words.

In writing practice the most efficient way to do this is to take a topic—what I remember of the sheep farm—and go. Not one time but over time do that assignment again and again till a full, rich picture appears. In between writings you might have to call your brother, a cousin to ask some specific questions or do some research, and then fold that new information also into the next writing.

I had the pleasure of helping to make the documentary *Tangled Up in Bob* with the filmmaker Mary Feidt. She shot more than a hundred hours of film but had to reduce it to one hour. In extracting a story line she had to be willing to let go of many terrific scenes and telling interviews. But no matter how good they were, if placed in the wrong place, they would have thrown off the story's intention and confused the viewer.

This is a good thing to be aware of as a writer—some of our greatest memories and writing finally won't fit the text and we have to let go of them—at least for now. Hopefully, they can find another place at another time. Let me warn you: you can avoid a lot of suffering by letting go and not trying to jam your darlings where they do not belong.

Tangled Up in Bob was a film about Bob Dylan's childhood on the Iron Range in northern Minnesota, but he and his music do not appear in the film. Sometimes you have to look not in the obvious places to find what you are looking for. If you go directly to the person and ask him who he is, often he is the least able to answer it. What seems the direct, obvious approach can get you lost.

A memoir is like a mirror reflecting back your life. But how to make the reflection true? You reach out in a lake and the moon's face ripples away. Or the way you see yourself is never how others see you. As you write deeply into your own life, there is so much you cannot grasp.

There are many ways to approach assembling your memoir. You want to keep in mind *structure,* which gives a frame around your memories. Then you pull the reader along by an enticement, a thin red line, a carrot on a stick. Often, like your plotless life, the allure is not obvious, but you keep on going anyway.

And you limit what you will cover for the particular work you are doing. You can't tell every minute of your life—or put in every darling experience. You can't eat everything on the table. You choose a portion, some fruit, vegetable, cheese, roast, cake, salad, and put it on your plate. You choose a time, a subject, a place, you give a shape to what is unruly. You lend it a form. The form is not a trick. It develops out of what you want to say and how you want to say it. Memoir is about you. If you are from Iowa you probably will have a different sensibility than someone from the Deep South or the West Coast.

Be who you are, relax, keep at it.

Vast

We write memoir not to remember, not to cling, but to honor and let go. Wave after wave splashes on the shore and is gone. Your mother once wore an embroidered Mexican peasant shirt, had gleaming teeth and a full head of black hair. She pushed the hammock you lay in, a million oak leaves above your head. You didn't yet know your first word. You were slow to learn to talk and your first step was as enormous as an elephant's. Her waist was below her blouse and you could hide in a voluminous maroon skirt. Sharp was the blue sky, the white porch steps.

Here's your mother now, frail at one hundred pounds, hearing aids plopped above her lobes, eyes a pale glaze seeing only form and shadow, in her own crooked way heading for another country.

Let her be as she is. You can't save her. You can only remember as she dissolves. With one arm you reach all the way back and with your other arm you steady the walker that she grasps before her.

But don't fool yourself. However old your mother is, you are always walking into vast rooms full of beginnings and endings, abundant with possibility. Try the empty cubicle of your page. What can you scratch in it before your turn comes to step up to the vast ocean all by yourself? Go. Ten minutes.

Over

What made you know something was over? Go. Ten minutes.

Turning Around

So who do you think you are writing this memoir for? Where does this urge come from? You will come up with many answers.

Consider this one: We are turning around to speak to our old selves—the ones from thirty years ago, the ones from two years past, the ones we thought were idiots, who failed, who won, who were petty, coy, bold, young, in love. We are finishing the circle, closing the gap, making sense of the senseless.

Who do we write for? our better, worse, encumbered, forfeited, imprisoned, beloved selves. *Jane, I am calling out to you. William, I am comforting you. Alberta, I won't forget you.*

We are waking up gorillas, alerting the hippos: we are coming. We exist and here's how we existed. The rocks are listening and the car part factories in Detroit are turning an ear toward us.

Natalie, you were good at thirty—pretty, too—but nothing like the owl shriek, goat climb, Barbary shore I am at sixty. I bow to the years between us, to your hip and kiss and step. To the aching you carried in your body, the hitchhiking to San Francisco where you met a woman who read *Moby Dick,* the Chinese man who bucked the draft. He wasn't going to kill Vietnamese, the same color as him. You met an architectural student, who loved to dance. You dragged yourself across beaches and terraces, hungry for something you couldn't find. Your hand became transparent from begging, your nails long and sharp. Remember the tequila you drank, the single can of beer in the back room. The vomit, the cold, how you slept under a heavy sky. Even California couldn't drain your restless blood. You could never love enough or know enough. I see you, I regard you. For a moment you are right here, my old friend from far away.

Now you try it: turn around, call back through the years—or months, or weeks. You see yourself learning algebra in seventh grade. A = B = C. Now you are D, outside that equation, but you remember how one letter can be equal and different than another. And you remember Henry down the street and Claire on the dirt road. And nothing that ever happened can be forgotten. To say forgive it is to whitewash it. It wasn't okay. It was better than that. It was what it was.

Go, ahead. Ten minutes. Direct your call straight down the wires. Write.

Not Take

What road did you not take and feel a small sigh about now? An industrial engineer, a reporter, a cowgirl?

What person did you not go out with who sometimes still flitters across your mind? It's okay. It's another way of exploring a road not taken. Go. Ten minutes.

Well

Who do you know that died well, in a way you want to emulate? Tell us about it.

Gore Vidal in his last memoir, *Point to Point Navigation,* writes of his companion of fifty years at Cedars-Sinai Medical Center in Los Angeles.

> As the nurse opened the door to the operating room where I could not follow, Howard turned to me in his wheelchair, and said, "Well, it's been great." Then the door closed behind him.

This twists the heart. So bare and unsentimental, it penetrates. We all want examples of how to die. We don't choose our death but we all need visions and examples of how to let go.

Zen teachers often wrote a last poem right before the Great Darkness. What do you have to say just before the shutter snaps shut?

Basho, the Japanese haiku master, with his students around him, pronounced the beginning verse of a haiku and then two different alternative lines for the end.

Which do you like better? he asked his disciples and closed his eyes, taking his last breath.

Guidelines and Suggestions
for Writing Memoir

Enter your memoir sideways, with little steps, not head-on.
   (p. 51)
Life is not linear; reflect and sort through the layers. (xix)
Embrace the crumbs with the cake (xvi)

The basics:
I remember/I don't remember
I'm looking at/I'm not looking at
I'm thinking of/I'm not thinking of (228)
Don't cross out. (2)
Keep the pen moving. (4)

Write economically with the elegance of math. (6)
Make your verbs alive. (95)
Use your senses. (8)
Get concrete. (43)
Stay detailed. (193)
Keep a list of topics. (38)

Lose control. (10)
Go for the jugular. (12)
Be willing to write with fear and danger at your side. (12)
Let go of trying to please or trying not to please. (31)
Build a tolerance for what you cannot bear. (12)

Guidelines and Suggestions for Writing Memoir

Write what's in front of your face. (35)
Listen to what is not said. (35)
Write about what was missing. (48)
Don't be logical. (52)
Find your own great—and crooked—path. (54)

Do some research. (193)
Be open to the world. (196)
Write what's really on your mind, what you really see, think, and feel. (61)
Don't try to make it pretty. (271)
Hang out in incongruity. Don't reject anything. (62)

Write down this sterling moment, just as it is. Then jot down other moments. (69–70)
The past can only be found in the present. (70)
Make each event, scene different. (179)
Show all the craziness full blast. (174)
Crack open sentences; break structure; slash through thoughts and the old order. (270)

Be resolute and at the same time be receptive. (97)
Don't get stuck where you haven't succeeded. Go on to something else. (212)
If monkey mind won't quiet down, let it rant for ten minutes. But stand your ground. (117)
Play with bold, restless, humorous and serious, positive and negative extremes. (144)
Not to immortalize but to surrender ourselves and give pleasure through stories. (147)
Build your house, brick by brick, each chapter separate but with integrity. (283)
Discover your organic structure. (286)

Trust your insides to lead you. (165)

Guidelines and Suggestions for Writing Memoir

Write what you are and what it is uniquely yours to do. (247)
Don't think. Write. (190)

Shut up and write. (186)
Slow down
Practice.

Some Great Memoirs to Read

These are culled from my favorites and from friends' favorites:

The Language of Baklava by Diana Abu-Jaber
Infidel by Ayaan Hirsi Ali
A Place to Stand by Jimmy Santiago Baca
A Long Way Gone by Ishmael Beah
Thank You and Okay! by David Chadwick
A Taco Testimony by Denise Chavez
Rock, Ghost, Willow, Deer by Allison Hedge Coke
My Mother's House and Sido by Colette
The Road from Coorain by Jill Ker Conway
Truth Serum by Bernard Cooper
Bones of the Master by George Crane
A Childhood by Harry Crews
The Black Notebooks by Toi Derricotte
An American Childhood by Annie Dillard
This House of Sky by Ivan Doig
Chronicles: Volume One by Bob Dylan
Miriam's Kitchen by Elizabeth Ehrlich
Waiting for Snow in Havana by Carlos Eire
Anne Frank: The Diary of a Young Girl by Anne Frank
The Meadow by James Galvin
The Thief's Journal by Jean Genet
The Little Virtues by Natalia Ginzburg
Fierce Attachments by Vivian Gornick
Bone Black by bell hooks

Some Great Memoirs to Read

Life Among the Savages by Shirley Jackson
The Autobiography of Malcolm X by Malcolm X
A Romantic Education by Patricia Hampl
When Heaven and Earth Changed Places by Le Ly Hayslip
A Moveable Feast by Ernest Hemingway
The Woman Who Watches Over the World by Linda Hogan
Dust Tracks on a Road by Zora Neale Hurston
Girl, Interrupted by Susanne Kaysen
My Brother by Jamaica Kincaid
French Lessons by Alice Kaplan
The Liars' Club by Mary Karr
The Woman Warrior by Maxine Hong Kingston
Operating Instructions by Anne Lamott
Survival in Auschwitz by Primo Levi
Walking with the Wind by John Lewis
Edge of Taos Desert by Mabel Dodge Luhan
West With the Night by Beryl Markham
Confessions of a Berlitz-Tape Chicana by Demetria Martinez
At Home in the World by Joyce Maynard
Red Azalea by Anchee Min
The Names by N. Scott Momaday
Becoming a Man by Paul Monette
The Dream of Water by Kyoko Mori
And When Did You Last See Your Father by Blake Morrison
Boomer by Linda G. Niemann
Speak, Memory by Vladimir Nabokov
The Same River Twice by Chris Offutt
Running in the Family by Michael Ondaatje
My Year of Meats by Ruth L. Ozeki
Truth & Beauty by Ann Patchett
Bead on an Anthill by Delphine Red Shirt
The Craggy Hole in My Heart and the Cat Who Fixed It by
      Geneen Roth
Patrimony by Philip Roth
While the Locust Slept by Peter Razor

Some Great Memoirs to Read

Always Running: La Vida Loca by Luis J. Rodriguez
Hunger of Memory by Richard Rodriguez
Burning the Days by James Salter
Naked by David Sedaris
Where Rivers Change Direction by Mark Spragg
My Indian Boyhood by Luther Standing Bear
Travels with Charley by John Steinbeck
The Farm on the River of Emeralds by Moritz Thomsen
Adventures in the Unknown Interior of America by Alvar Nuñez
    Cabeza de Vaca
The Glass Castle by Jeannette Walls
Talking Indian by Anna Lee Walters
Death of a Man by Lael Tucker Wertenbaker
Brothers and Keepers by John Edgar Wideman
Night by Elie Wiesel
Refuge by Terry Tempest Williams
Departures by Paul Zweig

Permissions

About the Author

Natalie Goldberg is an author, poet, teacher, and painter. She has written eleven books, including *Writing Down the Bones: Freeing the Writer Within* (1986), which has sold over a million and a half copies, is translated into fourteen languages, and started a revolution in the way we practice writing today. People from around the world attend her life-changing workshops and retreats, and she has a reputation of being a great teacher. With filmmaker Mary Feidt, she completed the documentary *Tangled Up in Bob*, about Bob Dylan's childhood on the Iron Range in northern Minnesota. Her lively paintings can be viewed at the Ernesto Mayans gallery on Canyon Road in Santa Fe. She currently lives in northern New Mexico. For more information, see her website: www.nataliegoldberg.com.